COLOURGENICS
AS BODY
LANGUAGE

COLOURGENICS AS BODY LANGUAGE

Steven John Culbert

W. Foulsham & Co. Ltd.
London • New York • Toronto • Cape Town •
Sydney

W. Foulsham & Company Limited
Yeovil Road, Slough, Berkshire, SL1 4JH

ISBN 0–572–01404–X

Printed in Great Britain by St. Edmundsbury Press,
Bury St Edmunds.

CONTENTS

To Jackie Simon

Sleek as a cat
My mystic queen
Here's a vow
That all have seen.

And be they yellow
Black, brown or white,
There sure to admire
Your soul's great fight.

That quelled the beast
And slayed the dragon
That ensures our souls
Shall meet in heaven.

INTRODUCTION

Why is it that we choose specific coloured clothes for ceremonial use? Why do we change out of perfectly good clothes before going out, having just spent hours getting into them? And why do we go off our favourite jumper for some unknown reason when someone would have had to fight to get it off our backs a month or so ago?

The reason is really quite simple. Our clothes vibrate to a colour, and that colour is a reflection of our inner selves — our soul's moods and emotions. The colours reflect the way we treat others, and the way we want to be treated ourselves, if only we knew how to understand and interpret what we see.

Psychics and mystics gifted with the ability to perceive and understand the aura have been using this method of colour divination for centuries. Yet more abundant in its usage is Nature in the animal and insect world, which has devised a method of colour coding that is used in many animal mating and feeding rituals to make sure that the animals can hunt, attract and mate with the correct species.

Even though many people may fail to recognise consciously the importance of colour in our lives, we are all blessed with the hidden subconscious, which is not only more in tune with our emotional and spiritual needs, but passes those needs on to our conscious mind by helping us decide what colours to wear and surround ourselves with in our daily lives. However, if we were able to bring this decision into the conscious, we would not only improve our ability to communicate our desires, emotions and intentions to others, but we would also help our spiritual evolution by recognising what we are to each other.

'Red to a bull' or 'red with rage' are two everyday sayings that we all use and relate to. We acknowledge red as a colour denoting excitement or aggressive energy, just as, in contrast, we lie by a calm blue sea on our holidays to relax and unwind. It is by extending and developing this subconscious understanding of colour and putting this knowledge to constructive use in our everyday lives that we gain the ability to control our own destinies, environments and emotions; elevating ourselves beyond the preconditioning of the system within which we must all exist.

The colours that we wear and choose to surround ourselves with in our homes and offices are the visible reflections of our invisible auras. As our emotions and desires change, our aura changes — invisibly to all but the trained eye. But anyone can see that we change the clothes we wear and the colours we choose. Having recognised this fact, it is simplicity itself for us all to begin to use the greatest language that we possess — the universal language of colour.

And this is where *Colourgenics* can help. This book will help you to develop the ability to train yourself to recognise the subsconscious messages your families, friends, workmates and associates are sending to you through their choice of colour. When you can interpret the messages the colours are sending, you can improve your understanding of others, and in turn their understanding of you, in the hope that we may all learn to co-exist in greater harmony.

1
THE HUMAN AURA

The first essential to understand is the nature of the human aura and its function in relation to our lives.

The human aura is known by many names — ethric, double soul, spirit, life force or magnetism to name but a few. It is in fact an electro-magnetic field surrounding the human body.

As a foetus in the womb, you are surrounded by the aura of your mother, and at birth you take a residue of that aura to sustain you through the trauma of birth. However, the moment you take your first voluntary breath of air from the cosmos around you, you begin to build your own auratic field, basic at first, but developing in strength as you grow into adulthood.

The energy source of the auratic field is shaped not only by the magnetic influence of our own sun and planets, but also by our relationship to our own planet, Earth.

Just as copper conducts electricity, so some rocks, minerals and environments conduct a stronger auratic field. Your environment therefore plays a significant part in the development of this energy field that surrounds the body.

The field of energy itself, in the average individual, extends from the body by up to a metre, and if you were able to see the field, it would appear as a slowly swirling, pulsing collection of tinted clouds which move around the physical body. Fractures, flaws or angry-looking spots that appear within this cloud are indicative of physical and mental stresses in the physical body

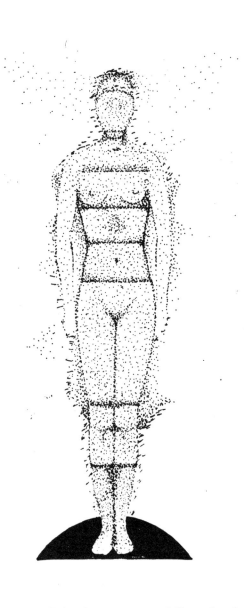

The HUMAN AURA   Appears as a swirling mist of tinted rather than definite colour that surrounds the human body

which, if left unattended, can develop into illnessess and depression.

Kirlion photography developed in the 1950s made it possible to photograph the aura itself along with its flaws, fractures and defects. Around this development has grown a band of practitioners and diviners who can be seen at the increasingly popular psychic and alternative health festivals. They will give an interpretation of the state of your aura.

It is not necessary to go to the expense of Kirlion photography, however to ascertain and interpret our aura. We all reflect the auratic field of our physical body in the colour, style and mode of our everyday clothes, and it is on this method of aura interpretation and development that we intend to concentrate in this book, as it is one which we can all see, and with a little patience and application can learn to read and interpret.

2
BASIC COLOURS

Before we go any further it is essential that we have a full understanding of the basic colours, our relationship to them, and how they can help or hinder our daily lives.

Colours themselves are best understood by the uninitiated when looked at in the light of their relationship with Nature. Nature's use of colour in the animal and insect world — whether it is as a warning, to attract a mate, or make the creative appear larger or smaller — is indeed a great indicator of the power of colour.

To understand the meaning of colour, we need to take a scientific look at the material properties of colour.

Sunlight

Colour in its true sense has its major source for us with the white light emitted by our own sun, which gives life to our planet Earth. White light is, in fact, a mixture of all the colours of the spectrum and is not in itself a real colour. It could perhaps more accurately be called a 'carrier' of colour, as is clearly demonstrated when water vapour acts as a prism to split the light into a multi-coloured rainbow.

With the use of a Spectroscope, astronomers have found the following chemicals and metals within this light.

The names of the metal elements are sodium, calcium, barium, magnesium, iron, chromium, nickel, copper, zinc, strontium, cadmium, cobalt, manganese, aluminium, titanium and rubidium. Hydrogen also exists within the sun's atmosphere and doubtless many more elements have something of their finer characteristics represented by light.

Broken down into the spectrum of colour, we find specific colours each contain different elements.

Materials of red light
Nitrogen, oxygen, barium, zinc, strontium, cadmium, and rubidium.

Materials of orange-red light
Hydrogen, oxygen, nitrogen, calcium, barium, iron, copper, strontium and cadmium.

Materials of orange light
Oxygen, calcium, iron, nickel, zinc, cobalt, aluminium, titanium and rubidium.

Materials of yellow light
Carbon, nitrogen, oxygen, calcium, barium, iron, chromium, titanium, aluminium, manganese, cobalt, cadmium, zinc, copper and strontium.

Materials in blue light
Barium, oxygen, nitrogen, titanium, aluminium, cobalt, manganese, cadmium, strontium, nickel, copper, zinc, chromium and magnesium.

Materials in green light
Iron, carbon, oxygen, nitrogen, calcium, cobalt, rubidium, manganese and titanium.

The rays of light from the sun find their expression in the trinity of elements hydrogen, nitrogen and oxygen. These, in turn, are vital constituents of many things on Earth, including all or large parts of sugars, gums, starches, ethers, alcohols, and many acids and plant substances. This clearly demonstrates how the elements of sunlight affect the very foliage and environment in which we live. It is its physical manifestation on this planet.

We can now proceed to examine the colours themselves and how they affect us.

White

As mentioned before, white is the carrier for the other colours of the spectrum and is therefore colour at its most complete and pure. White is the colour of completeness, purity and innocence. The seemingly barren Antarctic lies dormant awaiting the time when it may burst into life and activity with the ebb and flow of the polar caps. The bride at the altar dressed in white is affirming her chastity and loyalty in the vows of wedlock. The hospital doctor wears a crisp white overall as he goes about his rounds healing, helping and assisting those in need of his knowledge.

White is, in fact, the colour of the creation the womb, the book of knowledge as yet unopened, the seed or egg from which all things are born. White merely awaits you as creator to extract your needs from within its womb.

Red

Red is primarily a colour of energy and expansion. It has the ability to build constructively or to tear down, dependent upon how you direct its energy. It is the colour of the sexual expression of man that can on the positive side create life, though its baser use is destructive anger and the colour of war.

Red in excess can be a great causer of stress, and too much leads to an excess of energy which can turn into anger and aggression leading to breakdown of reasoning. It is, however, a good colour to surround yourself with if you are feeling run down or tired, as it assists you to summon your reserves of physical energy in order to accomplish the task at hand.

When our sun has violent solar storms, the red spectrum flares, and a similar phenomenon happens with Man. The adage 'red with rage' was not born from nothing, but rather from the perceived energy release sensed by those in proximity when someone lost his temper. Negative red energy is destructive, as it has no true direction or control.

Pink

Pink is the mixture of red and white, or white reflecting the subtle side of red. The sexual expression is softened into a need to care for and to protect. Pink is the colour of true love, expressing the desire to share one's energies, emotions and feelings. It is the colour of compassion and warmth when in its lighter pastel shades, though it can be more base and physically oriented in its darker shades. (The sexual organs of man and woman are a dark pink).

Pink is usually considered a feminine colour, however if more men were to make use of the softer energies of pink, the outdated need to establish his masculinity would be overcome and men would develop by leaps and bounds, overcoming their feelings of inadequacy in our overcompetitive world.

Pink is mainly a colour of emotional and physical love, and relationships built on pink vibrations are far superior to the mainly physical red relationships. For, whether we like it or not, sex is not the only thing that makes us attractive to our fellow humans and a relationship based solely on physical attraction is doomed to eventual failure.

Orange

Orange is a mixture of red and yellow, red being the physical energy and yellow the mental, therefore orange is the colour of projected or assertive mental energy. Orange in its darker shades can make the mental energy too rigid in its ideals and direction — a bit like a bull in a china shop — as it leans too much towards the physical energy of red. The lighter the orange, the more the yellow has control, and this can make them too logical in their approach to the problems and tasks at hand. The best shade of orange is a blend of the two, combining the mind and body into a vibration that has the ability to work tirelessly until it has achieved their objectives.

Orange would be a good colour to decorate schools and colleges, as it would bring out the best abilities in the students.

Yellow

Yellow is the colour of knowledge and mental activity. It is the colour of logic and learning, mental growth and the stimulation of the higher mind. Since Man first looked up at the yellow sun and pondered its warmth and light, it set alight in him the desire to learn.

Too much yellow can make you too dictatorial on the mental plane, which creates rigidity in ideology and stunts the ability for real mental expansion. Different shades of yellow show the level of mental activity present; the lighter the yellow the purer the thought process, the darker the shade the more physical it can become.

Green

In Nature, green is the colour of foliage the gatherer of energy from the sun, self-healing and regenerating. In the aura, it is the colour of physical growth and healing. Green is a restful colour which allows us the time to rest and replenish our reserves of energy in order that we may enter our next phase of growth.

Yellow-green or luminous green are sometimes referred to as the energy of occult power, though my own personal belief is that the creative recycling properties have been misinterpreted. Green is the colour of regeneration, rest and repair.

Brown

In Nature, growth stems from the brown soil. It is the energy reserves of Nature and encompasses the physical elements for the growth of green.

Brown is therefore the colour of material security and wealth, but just as green growth turns brown and returns in cycle to re-nurture new green growth, so the material wealth and prosperity of brown in the material world must be reintroduced into the society from whence it came.

Brown is therefore a colour for regeneration of material prosperity. It should be put to constructive use and not hoarded lest your land or wealth become barren.

Blue

Blue in Nature is the colour of the sky and the sea. Blue is the colour of mystery and awakens the emotional feelings of Man. From the first time he looked up in wonder at the sky or pondered the vastness of the oceans, he kindled his desire to seek the unknown. The darker the shade of blue, the more mystery it contains, while the lighter it grows, ending in pastel shades, the more understanding it has become. The reasoning behind this is that pastel blue fades to the completeness of white and is able to absorb more blue, while dark blue is on the edge of purple, which represents spirituality.

Blue-greens, such as turquoise, bring about the desire for spiritual growth after contemplation and are ideal colours for those with important decisions to make.

Violet/Purple

Violet is the colour of spiritual growth, philosophy and royalty. I include royalty as they are normally the spiritual leaders of their people or head of their country's religion. The darker the shade of purple, the more secretive are its actions and the lighter the shade the more it is able to express itself. Purple is a mixture of the energy of red and the emotion of blue, and gives the aura the energy to transcend the material and enter the spiritual realms of life. It is the colour of the higher side of Man and is a common ceremonial colour in religious sects and royal families.

Black

Black is not really a colour at all, but is in fact an opposite to white and another carrier of colour. If you mix all colours together you achieve black. It is, however, a colour of secrets and the unknown, for black is also the last visible colour before the invisible colours such as ultra-violet and infra red. Black is therefore a colour which hides things, be they good or bad. Black itself is not evil, it is the use which we put it to — a plump woman may wear black to appear thinner, just as a skinny woman can wear black to appear larger.

It is a colour of apprehension and yet its very existence can guard against or hide that which we fear. Black can be the colour of the alter ego, our Jekyll and Hyde, but our inner selves are as good or as bad as we make them, as we are the creators of our own black thoughts.

Warm and Cold Colours

One important point to note is that colours are often referred to as being warm or cold. The warm colours are red, pink, yellow and orange and are said to be active and assertive, while the cold colours are blue, purple, violet and brown, said to be passive and emotional.

This leaves poor old green as the pig in the middle, as it has the warmth of yellow coupled to the coldness of blue, and is a bridge between the two. Whether the sectioning is valid or not still remains to be proven to me. I do, however, agree that the positive sides of the warmer colours bring out the more pleasurable memories.

White could be considered the warm side and black the cold as they relate to day and night, neither is really a colour, more a carrier of colour.

Though we place no great emphasis on this sectioning, it is another clue to assist us in our interpretation of the overall effect of the colours that we wear.

3
COLOURS AND THEIR ASTROLOGICAL LINKS

As well as having links with the elements, colours also have specific links with astro-numbers, gemstones, birthsigns and other important astrological phenomena.

The following table shows how these relate to indivual colours.

Colour	Stone	Planet	Metal	Astro-number	Birth-sign
White	Diamond	Sun	Gold	1	Leo
Scarlet Indigo	Beryl Jasper	Mercury	Mercury	5	Virgo Gemini
Red	Malachite Ruby	Mars Pluto	Sodium	9	Scorpio Aries
Green	Emerald Lapiz Lazuli	Venus	Copper	6	Taurus Libra
Blue	Amethyst	Neptune	Tin	7	Pisces
Black	Sapphire	Saturn	Lead	8	Capricorn
Silver	Pearl	Moon	Silver	2	Cancer
Orange	Opal	Uranus	Uranium	4	Aquarius
Purple	Topaz	Jupiter	Tin	3	Sagittarius

How Colours Relate to Gemstones, Planets, Metals, Astro-numbers and Birthsigns

4
AREAS OF THE BODY

For the purpose of interpretation and analysis we are going to divide the body into five areas of garments which are as follows:

the upper inner body;
the upper outer body;
the lower inner body;
the lower outer body;
undergarments.

These sections will then be divided into the conscious and subconscious expressions of the wearer as follows:

the upper inner body . . . subconscious emotional;
the upper outer body . . . conscious emotional;
the lower inner body . . . subconscious physical;
the lower outer body . . . conscious physical;
undergarments . . . sexual behaviour and inner self.

Clothing divisions

The upper inner body contains the following garment types: vests, shirts, blouses, T-shirts and so on.

The upper outer body contains the following garment types: hats, coats, jackets, jumpers, cardigans and so on.

The lower inner body contains the following garment types: socks, tights and stockings, longjohns and so on.

The lower outer body contains the following garment types: shoes, footwear, trousers, skirts and so on.

The underwear section is to include all underwear which makes full contact with the skin such as bras and briefs, Y-fronts and so on.

Accessories such as jewellery, scarves, ties and belts will be discussed in a separate section, as they have a different overall effect on the colour vibration of the wearer.

The Upper Body

The upper body contains the movement above the waist and that of the arms and head as well as the vocal chords which are our main medium of communication.

The upper body represents the conscious way in which we express ourselves and relate to each other, and it includes the parts of the body that give us most control over our environment. One would think that it would therefore relate to the physical, but this is not really so. The brain which controls our ability to think, philosophise and dream is also the centre which controls the emotions, while the sexual, regenerative organs of the lower body rule the area which creates physical life. So it is the upper body which controls the ability to reflect, consciously or subconsciously, our emotional state and feelings.

We have divided the upper body section into two parts because we believe that the outer garments reflect the emotional conditions we feel able to deal with at the time of wearing the colours; the inner colours of the upper body reflect the emotional situations or environments we would like to exist, but lack the knowledge or confidence to create.

It must also be remembered that the outer clothing which hangs from the upper body, such as jackets and coats, not only protect us from inclement weather but give us the emotional security to venture out into the elements.

Another important argument which supports our researched, tried-and-tested theory is that desire, love, hate and greed are all emotions which are expressed through movements of the upper body whether it be in an embrace or a shaken fist.

The Lower Body

As you will have already gathered from the previous page, the lower body is a reflection of our physical selves and our material needs. The movement from the waist down encompasses us with not only the regenerative sexual organs but also the parts of our body which carry us into new environments or away from difficult ones.

Again we have divided this section into two parts, that of the physical way we relate to our surroundings and of how we would like our surroundings to be but have not yet ventured into.

Communication between the Upper and Lower Body

Both upper and lower body communicate their individual requirements to each other. This helps them to overcome the problems each may encounter. For example, the arms may have to take over from the feet when the water becomes too deep for the legs to wade any further. So it is when you look at the colours that your subjects or yourselves are wearing, each has its own home but can help or hinder its opposite if it is not in tune.

The upper body is perhaps 70 per cent emotional and

30 per cent, physical while the reverse is so of the lower body, but always bear in mind that this is not an absolute rule but is indicative of the energies at play.

Underwear

Underwear has been separated from the upper and lower clothing sections and given a section of its own because it falls into both, and yet is neither. It is the clothing which is our last barrier before the sexual act, as well as being the garments closest to the skin. It is usually seen, in fact, only by those whom we trust enough to be that personal with and is by colour our emotional and physical souls combined.

Because these garments are our last shield and barrier from emotional embarrassment, as well as being a reflection of our inner physical selves to our chosen mates or partners, I have given it a section to itself.

Try not to giggle and make light of this section, but look at it in the opposite way it has been written, for it holds the answer to your emotional and physical needs and inhibitions, and is perhaps the most important section in this book. Only by recognising what is missing in your life can you hope to include it and find the harmony which you have so long sought.

Accessories

One other minor section at the end of the dictionary deals with accessories. These are really lanterns or indicators which you use to attract attention to a colour or tone you are already wearing and will be dealt with as such.

5
MALE AND FEMALE COLOURS

Some colours are said to be male and others female, just as some are said to be warm and others cold. The female colours are the pastel shades, while the male colours could be said to be the darker shades of any colour. We all know the convention that baby boys are dressed and decorated in blue, and girls in pink. Why is this so? Pink expresses the open warmth with which girls may show all of their passive emotional feelings, while the blue of the male is already restricting him from showing his.

Colours are, in fact, neither masculine nor feminine. It is merely the social preconditioning which man imposes, so he can recognise or feel safer with his own environment, that causes colours to be categorised in this way.

We are all, of course, a part of the social conditions in which we live. While colour can reflect those conditions, it is our acceptance or non-acceptance of them as adults when under our own control and direction that shows whether or not we become the individuals we would like to be, or merely sheep following the flock. The colours we wear in relation to masculinity and femininity are reflections of our acceptance or non-acceptance of social stereotypes.

This does not mean that all men should rush out and buy pink clothes or women blue ones in order to assert their individuality. But it does mean that they should recognise the colour for what it really represents and endeavour to introduce it into their surroundings or decor if they feel comfortable with it. The society a man lives in allows him to interact with pink vibrations when his wife or partner wears them, so it is not necessary for him actually to wear pink, nor women blue.

The essential is that we can, if we really want to, find outlets for our colour vibrations — be they considered male or female — without being embarrassed by how we feel others will react.

The gay gentleman with the pink hair and poodle is probably a lot braver that you or I, as he makes full use of his environmental colour vibration to express his emotional and physical needs to others, even if it is a little blatant. His use of pink to show those feelings is only a reflection of the warmth and compassion he feels the need to give to others; it does not, however, make him weak or mentally abnormal. That is the direction given by the society in which he lives, and which cannot understand why a man can need to be so openly compassionate and giving.

The same is also true of the women who need to wear the so-called masculine colours and garment types.

Before we end our brief look at sexing the colours, it is important to note our belief that the gay community, which is becoming increasingly public, is not something which could have existed had people understood how to accept all emotions, whether reflected through colour or not. A gay woman would have found her physical opposite in an emotional man, just as a gay man would have found his expression through an assertive woman. However, neither of these conditions was acceptable in societies of the past, so the hidden feelings and emotions had to find an outlet within the same gender — and that puts us all at fault.

Wear the colours you feel attracted to. They do not state that you are "male" or "female", and they certainly do not mean you are gay. They merely express your need for others to look at you in the way which you wish to be seen, not in the way your social preconditioning would have you believe they see you.

DICTIONARY
OF CLOTHES
AND COLOURS

Before beginning any actual interpretations of the colours of the clothes you and your associates wear, it is important to understand that the individual colours of particular garments are in themselves only parts of the whole picture. If you find a bruised banana in your shopping, you do not judge the whole batch to be rotten, but merely cut away the bad part and eat the remainder.

So it is with our interpretation of the overall needs of our subjects. Each piece of clothing is inter-related to those around it. All the clothes should be interpreted as contributing to the overall picture.

Look for the most dominant overall colour; this is the basic key or message your subject is trying to put across. From that point on, judge the relation the other colours make upon the dominant colour by both position and tone or shade. Look upon the colours of any accessories as being beacons of tone that highlight or complement the key garment colours. And remember that some colours mix well, while others do not, just as certain emotions can be creative or destructive when displayed in conjunction with others.

Remember that inner garments relate to the inner desires of our nature, while outer garments relate to the energy with which we feel safer and more secure, or which we wish to attract to ourselves.

The upper body colours will have more effect on emotional desires, while the lower body colours relate more to physical and material needs.

Take all these factors into account and try to be in tune with nature in how you assess the way in which the colours mix and blend with each other. Nature gives us the key to unlock our understanding of its own system by our very surroundings and its own interaction with itself.

Last but not least, try to be objective. Remember that the conclusions you reach about the colours someone else is wearing can be influenced by the colours you yourself are wearing. Try to separate your own emotional and physical perception of your colours from those you are interpreting.

So, having fixed these points firmly into your mind, you are now able to proceed with the dictionary itself.

Make use of this chart for quick basic direction of colour meanings, but remember to blend them into an overall picture.

Shoes, boots footwear.	Conscious recognition of safe areas that you feel the need to control.
Socks, stockings, legwear.	Subconscious energy of safe areas that you would like to control.
Trousers, skirts etc.	Conscious direction in which your physical self would like to go.
Shirts, Vests, blouses etc.	Subconscious direction of emotional energies.
Jumpers, Coats, jackets etc.	Conscious emotional feelings that you feel able to express and share.
Accessories	Tones and shades which draw attention to other energies that you wear.
Underwear	Sexual expression and inner self.

FOOTWEAR

When you look at your subject's feet, remember to take into account the shape of the shoes as indicative of the degree of expression the individual feels comfortable with.

Those who wear high pointed shoes tend to be the types who set out to impress, but can be sharp-tongued or retreat from criticism of their actions. They are also likely to take more risks than other types.

People who wear flat pointed shoes need a firm base from which to operate before they actually enact the many tasks they talk about doing one day. They are, however, a little more practical than the high-heeled type.

Those who choose flat square shoes are the most practical of all, needing both a reason for what they are doing as well as company or support to back them up should things go wrong. They make very loyal companions and are reliable friends when you need assistance.

People who favour boots can be interpreted in a similar way, but they do require that little bit more protection or security before they venture out. However, once set upon a course of action, boot types are much harder to stop.

Pumps, sports shoes and the like are indicative of the type of person who may look comfortable and relaxed but is in fact not as reliable as they would have us believe. They are always ready for a quick get-away should the need arise and can be impatient or impractical.

Sandals are indicative of a more relaxed type of person, as they are both practical and relaxed. While this may be a good thing in some situations, it also shows that the wearer is not keen on the fast lane activities or stresses of the society in which they live. It may indicate the desire to let others take on the responsibilities for those things which the wearer has neither the time nor the energy to accomplish.

All shoe types cannot be instantly slotted into one box or another and it is up to you as analyst to decide which type of shoes your subject is wearing in order that it may be applied to the colour meaning.

Shoe Colours

White, red, pink, yellow, orange, green, blue, brown, purple, black

White

White shoes express a more puritanical outlook for the physical direction. There is a desire for a complete and total answer to the physical problems and situations in which the wearer is involved. People who wear a lot of white shoes want to be admired but not touched, for fear of feeling out of their depth. They can be rigid in their ideology or outlook and need to soften their image if they are to join the mainstream of society.

Red

Red shoes show a desire for change in the physical direction. They show the desire to bring the physical and sexual energy under control, as it has no real direction or course at this time. If you wear a lot of red shoes, you feel the need for more physical contact and interaction with your chosen mate, partner or associates and should tell them so if you are to maintain your equilibrium.

Pink

Pink shoes reveal the physical desire to express your feelings of love, loyalty and compassion that may be unnoticed by your partner. Or they may convey the message to others that you are available and able to interact if you had a suitable partner. It is an excellent colour for people to wear and shows others that you have the ability both to give and take on a physical level. The lighter the pink, the more mental is the interaction and the darker the shade, the more the needs are towards physical contact and reassurance.

Yellow

Yellow shoes express the logical or mental direction under which you have placed your physical need. You try too hard to make things happen, and may be mistrustful of other people's motives, always needing to know the underlying reason why. If you often wear yellow shoes, you keep too much control over your physical actions. You could miss out on a lot of fun unless you learn to take others for what they are, rather than for the logical machines you would at times like them to be. You may need to keep yourself under control in order to feel safe, but others around you may want to let their hair down. Yellow shoes may be good at work, but should be taken off if you are to enjoy your play.

Orange

Orange is the mixture of the physical energy of red and the logical energy of yellow. It expresses the wearer's desire to mix the qualities of the two and find an outlet for them. Orange worn on the feet should be considered a warning to others. It is stating that the wearer is fed up with present conditions, and is looking for and planning a new course of action which will bring about the changes that he or she desires. People who wear orange shoes can be at that time more forceful in their interaction with others, and you should avoid confrontations.

Green

Green shoes are the neutral ground of footwear, being neither warm nor cold, aggressive nor passive. Green is Nature's colour of the medium between the brown of the soil and the blue of the sky; or the logic of yellow and the emotion of blue. It is a healing colour, and if you wear green shoes you are trying to heal or overcome physical problems by growing out of the needs you once had, or by repairing that which you were. If you often wear green shoes, you are allowing others to use you as an emotional and physical doormat for their problems. Take some time off and do the things you want to do — you can't sit on the fence for ever.

Blue

Blue shoes are worn at a time when we are under a degree of emotional instability. The desire is to find a physical direction for unused or misused emotional feelings. Blue heals emotional scars, and when you wear blue shoes you are trying to bring into the open, face up to and conquer the emotional instability in your life. The paler the blue, the more time you require, and the more reassurance you need to express those feelings. The darker the blue, the greater is the intensity of your understanding of the emotional needs of others and the ability to supply what they require in order to exist physically within your environment. If you often wear blue shoes, you fear to commit your emotions in a physical relationship.

Brown

Brown shoes are an expression of the desire to have more control over and to obtain more financial stability in the wearer's physical life. The brown soil of Nature contains all the nutrients and elements for growth. It releases these to plants to allow them to grow, as well as providing a secure base to grow from. People who wear brown shoes need more material wealth and security before they feel confident and at ease with their fellow men. It is not that they are inadequate or insecure, but more that they need to have something to have and hold and so prove to themselves that they have achieved success.

Purple

Purple shoes are worn by people who seek to elevate themselves beyond the physical and into the spiritual. The colour brings out the philosopher in Man, and when worn as footwear it shows that the wearer is trying to bring under control his desire to get out of the rat race of daily life and find a more peaceful or less stressful environment. Purple is a colour that is worn by those seeking a more spiritual answer to the physical problems surrounding them. They rarely resort to physical aggression as a solution to their problems. If you often wear purple shoes, you are in danger of alienating yourself from the realities of the society in which you exist.

Black

Black is probably the most common colour for shoes in society today. Black is the colour of mystery. Its association with sex is strong only because we treat the subject with such a degree of mystery and are loth to discuss it openly with others. Black shoes in reality indicate that you have no real physical direction as yet, and are still testing your surroundings in order to wake up and become what you find enjoyable.

Black hides all the invisible colour spectrum and those who wear black shoes all the time feel the need to hide a part of themselves away from others lest they be rejected or ridiculed. If you often wear black shoes, you are a little unsure of how to deal with your physical expression and how others would react to it. As a result, you pretend to be something you are not, in the hope that others will not recognise your insecurity. If you were to relate and express your desires to friends and associates, you would find more than a sympathetic ear. We all have the same phobias and fears to one degree or another, and are merely waiting for others to recognise them in us and help us to overcome them.

CONCLUSION

Remember your shoes are the part of our clothing which keep us in contact with, yet protect us from the Earth we live on. They are expressions of our ability to feel physically secure.

SOCKS, STOCKINGS AND LEGWEAR

Socks, Stockings and Legwear

The energies reflected by these garments are expressions of the direction we would like to take in our physical lives, but have either not done so or not recognised the need to, at the time of wearing the colours. The socks and stockings are inner expressions of the shoes that have not yet found the outlet they seek. It is a subconscious physical indicator of what we desire to bring under control in the near future. If our shoes keep us firmly planted on the ground, then it is the socks and stockings which soften the blow of the terrain the shoes cover.

Socks on men are the only visible reflection of lower inner garments, just as stockings are on women. And it is this flash of colour that gives us an insight into the inner personality of our subject's ability to change or accept their physical lifestyles.

Women's tights and nylons are more available in more colours than ever before, just as women have become more outspoken about their status in society. The mundane blacks and shades of brown are long gone, and with the new range of colours at their disposal women have become more confident in their desire to express their own inner needs and emotions.

Socks and Stocking Colours

White, red, pink, yellow, orange, green, blue, brown, purple, black

White

White socks and stockings show that wearers are hiding most of their true feelings of physical expression behind a façade of purity. White contains all colours, but has not yet been formed into a colour of its own. The meaning here is that you fear others will not see you as you wish to be seen, or that you have an inner conflict of emotion that you wish to overcome by yourself before you feel able to give to others. The inner self is not yet ready to give of itself when this colour is worn here.

Red

Red socks and stockings show the wearer has an excess of inner energy that has not yet found a physical direction. The red energy is being bottled up and needs to find a way of escaping before it turns into anger or depression. More physical contact is desired by the wearer from friends, partners and associates, but the tap can't find a way to turn itself on and release the energy.

If you wear lots of garments of this colour you wish to expand more, do more and see more, but may be held back by your environment. It is a subconscious message to your associates that you are more independent than they may think, and want to be a part of what is going on around you.

If your mate wears this colour he or she is usually more ready to interact on a physical level.

Pink

Pink socks and stockings are indicative of the inner warmth and compassion the wearer feels for those around them or who are associated to them at that time. It is a message of the inner peace you feel within yourself and would like to share with others, if only they stopped for long enough to see that you are prepared to give your all.

You have found a physical direction that you feel confident with and are able to share with people who are special and important to you. If you wear this colour garment, you want to interact with those close to you, but are unsure how to go about it and need them to start the ball rolling or notice what you have to offer.

Pink is a warm sympathetic colour that shows the wearer is prepared to share everything but only with those who are prepared to give as good as they get.

Yellow

Yellow socks and stockings are worn by those who are pondering upon and seeking answers to their lack of physical interaction. The mental energy of yellow logic has taken over the inner physical self to seek the answers for its lack of physical expression. If you wear this garment colour a lot, you have withdrawn from interaction with others and may be seeking self assurance in the way you live. It may be that at this time you are fed up with the way have been treating you and are undergoing a period of reassessment of your circumstances. It may also mean you know the way you would like your life to be, but cannot put it into action. Either way, it is a message to others that your patience is growing thin, and your inner self is about to reach a decision on which it will act.

Orange

Orange socks and stockings have mixed the logic of yellow with the energy of red in order to cope with an inner shyness, and project the wearer's ideals and ambitions into physical reality. The darker the shade, the more control the red energy has over the mental yellow. The lighter the shade, the more logical is the answer to the problem. The colour shows that the wearer feels he has thought enough and intends to act with or without the support of his friends or associates.

Orange as an energy can build or destroy, so tread carefully if your partner wears this colour, as their patience is like thin ice and could swallow you up at any time. An angry sun flashes shades of yellow and orange, and garments here can be indicators of a storm of protest that is about to erupt upon those who have offended.

Green

Green socks and stockings are worn at a time when you feel the need for inner rest and tranquility. You may have been through a period of physical or emotional hard work and need the time oft to rest, re-orientate and direct your future actions. Green is the colour of healing, and when worn in these garment types indicates the need to lick your inner wounds and prepare yourself for the next round.

The mixture of the blue emotion and the mental yellow have combined so that you may strengthen your inner resolve to accomplish your inner desire, but only if you are allowed the chance to rest. Garments of this colour worn here show that you are not at your physical best, and require the time and understanding of your associates while you rest and recuperate in order that you may take up the banner anew with the dawn.

Blue

Blue garments of this type are indicators of the wearer's lack of ability to express or achieve emotional desires.

As an inner garment colour, blue is indicative of bottled up or suppressed emotional energy seeking a physical means of expression which it has yet to find, or is being inhibited in its expression of these desires. No colour is actually good or bad, but is rather an indicator of the level of types of energy that we are either expressing with ease, or are failing to communicate to others.

Blue is a very emotional colour that shows itself either when we are repairing and regenerating our emotions, or when they are at such an excessive level that we are unable to communicate or find an outlet for them. Any inner garment reflects more of our subconscious desires, or limitations that we have either imposed upon ourselves or are forced to live under because of the limitations of our environment. This in itself is a self-imposed environment, as we can change either the limitations of our surroundings by expressing our true emotional needs, or move on and physically change our surroundings if they do not comply with our desires. The choice is ours.

Blue garments worn on this part of the body should be read as a warning to those around the wearer that they desire a physical change either in the way they are emotionally treated in their environment, or in how they wish to receive more reassurance of the physical safety of that environment. If this is not forthcoming, then the wearer will eventually direct the energy to where they feel reassured, which is as far away as possible from where they felt insecure. When worn only occasionally, the wearer is reassessing his physical emotional standing and relationships with those in the immediate environment and may tend to be a little bit more depressed or tired at the time of wearing such garments.

Brown

Brown socks and stockings are worn at a time when we are more concerned with our material wellbeing. Brown is the colour of the soil which contains all the riches required for growth, but has either not yet put its riches to use or is saving them for better times.

If you wear a lot of brown socks or stockings you have a subconscious need to feel financially or materially stable before you are able to commit yourself to or become to involved in emotional relationships.

You need to gather your resources on the material plane in order to compete on the physical plane.

Brown is not a greedy colour. It is, in fact, the nutrient supplier of Nature, capable of supporting great harvest if you know how to till its soil. If you find you wear this colour a lot, think hard of instances in your life when you have wanted to commit yourself to projects or relationships, but did not do so because you felt you had neither the resources nor material stability to project your dreams — or so you thought at that time. Brown wearers can be important in institutions or charities, but tend to put back only what they feel they owe to their society or environment.

Purple

Purple symbolises philosophy, regality, spirituality and the higher consciousness of Man. When worn as an inner garment colour of this type, it is a reflection of the inner thought process to which the wearer is their subject. You are less physically active or assertive when you wear this colour, and are more likely to be considering or planning future phases of, or current circumstances of, your physical and spiritual well being.

The paler the purple, the stronger the desire to

cleanse yourself of some facet of your physical surroundings. The darker the shade, the more difficult the enactment of your problem has become.

Purple garments of this type indicate the subconscious desire for a change in the ways you either physically react with others, or the way you want others to see you. Its association with religion and royalty endorses the fact that the wearer wants to care about his physical surroundings, but at the time of wearing such garments is unable to do so openly. If you wear socks and stockings of this colour only occasionally, then it reflects your emotional need to find a physical outlet for your higher self, which you may feel is going unnoticed by those close to you. It is also indicative of those who wish to care for or help someone or some cause but have not yet found one worthy of their energies. The overall effect of this garment colour is a frustrated or unfulfilled outlet for the higher mind.

Black

Black, as already stated, is not a colour but a carrier of all the invisible colours. It hides within itself a brilliant rainbow that is hidden from the eyes of men.

When worn as an inner garment of this type it shows that the wearer either has something to hide or has not yet found the physical surroundings in which it may interact on a secure level. Black states that it has not yet decided on the direction it should take or where its loyalties lie. When worn on the feet, as in socks and stockings, on a regular basis, it is an indicator that the wearer is apt to change his mind or ideals without warning. It also shows that his loyalties are to the people he is with at the time, but as quickly as the people change, so can those loyalties.

People who wear this colour a lot are neither weak

nor misdirected. They are following others with the express purpose of finding something into which they can direct their own physical energies, but with the knowledge that, when they have found that direction, they can break cleanly with the old and live for the new. Black on the lower inner body worn only on occasions is indicative of periods of boredom when the wearer wants to find a new avenue of excitement but has not yet done so.

On the negative side, black socks and stockings are worn to create an air of mystery which we may use to attract others in order to excite ourselves. But only rarely do we give back in return what we take. Who knows what lurks beyond the inner darkness of a cave, and who is truly brave enough to venture in without a light?

TROUSERS AND SKIRTS

White, red, pink, orange, yellow, green, brown, purple, blue, black

The colour of outer clothing on the lower body, such as trousers and skirts, are reflections of our physical defences and moods. Just as the outer walls of a fort repel the initial onslaught of attackers, so do outer lower garments indicate the energies to which we are more defensive, or the way in which we will react to physical pressure.

On the positive side, they are an expression of the physical energy that the wearer has in excess, and is capable of utilising should the opportunity present itself — be that to defend or attack. This garment type should not be read solely on its own colour, but also in conjunction with the colours above and below it — the shoes and shirt — as these are also indicators of the direction of the physical energy, both in its strength and positive (warm) or negative (cold) state.

White

White trousers and skirts worn on a regular basis other than for sport are worn by a type of person who is self-critical to extremes. But people who are self-critical are also apt to be quickly critical of others, so beware.

White is the pure carrier of the visible light spectrum, and although it may look bright and clear, it quickly tarnishes or soils when brought into contact with its physical surroundings. White garment wearers of this type want to be admired and respected for their physical beauty or achievement but don't want others to get too close lest it spoil their image, or challenge their feelings of superiority on which they build their emotional stability.

Wearers of white garments on the outer lower body are, on the other hand, a little more active and adaptable than the rest of us. They can become what is required of them in order to achieve the admiration that they both live for and desire.

If you wear this colour only occasionally, then it is an expression of your desire to be recognised for yourself and your own achievements, rather than for those of your mates of your surroundings. It is an indicator that you wish to assert yourself more on your physical surroundings; receive recognition for physical achievements; or just attract more attention to yourself because you feel you have recently been neglected.

Red

Red trousers or skirts are worn at a time when we have an excess of positive or negative physical energy or desire for which we are seeking an outlet. If you often wear red trousers or skirts you are indicating to others that you are ready and available for more physical sexual interaction, either because your mate has neglected you or just because you feel in the mood.

It is also a negative indicator that you are fed up with your current partner or mate, who, you feel, does not notice or appreciate your physical offerings. You are prepared to accept bids from others who can give you the physical interaction and security that you desire.

Red is not just a colour of sexual activity. It reflects the physical way in which we progress through our lives, and should be read in conjunction with the colours around it to ascertain its true direction. Red can be a very destructive force either upon the wearer or those who oppose them, but once unleashed it is one of the hardest energies to control.

If you wear red skirts and trousers only occasionally, then you are trying to communicate to your surroundings that you are feeling the need to be more adventurous and active, and need someone with to whom share that energy.

The legs are the limbs of the body which take us about our daily lives — whether to advance and progress or retreat and consolidate. When we wear red on the lower outer body, the red energy is looking for a conscious direction for these energies to flow back or forth. The only problem is that the red energy is volatile and destructive if it is halted or obstructed in its direction, and will be quick to anger, and to retreat or advance its direction and ideals. So be warned and learn to flow with the tide of red, as opposing it may bring about your destruction.

Red garment wearers want fun and physical interaction. However, they are overly defensive of their environments or emotions when they wear this colour with blue, for example. So remember to take the surrounding colours into account when assessing red trousers and skirts. The bull quietly grazes the pasture till he sees the red flag that encourages him to greater physical activity. Once set in motion, he is enraged until the source of his anger is removed or his life is ended by the sword. Try not to anger people who wear this garment colour, as they are more apt to fly off the handle and lose their tempers when they wear this garment colour. Red is a colour which expresses the wearers' desire to be more physically active in their surroundings and is worn on the lower outer body at a time when we have a higher level of physical energy.

Pink

Pink trousers and skirts are worn at a time when we feel more physically at ease with our surroundings. The warmth and compassion of the colour pink, reflected through the conscious physical parts of the body, states that the wearer feels at peace with or has something to give to their physical environment.

The pure physical energy of red has combined with the purity of white to find a direction and become demonstrative of its feelings of warmth, compassion and security. This colour worn on the lower outer body is rarely negative, for even in its negativity it has positive aspects. If you wear this colour on the negative side it still shows your desire for a peaceful physical interaction with someone you can love, or the ability or desire to share with others the better side of your nature. It is then up to them to recognise and interact with you. The lighter the pink, the more control the wearer has over the ability to control the physical feeling. The darker the shade becomes, the more the emotions become involved in the physical decisions we all have to make.

If you often wear this colour on the outer lower body, you are expressing your ability to share with others all that you possess, should you find them worthy of your trust. You are indicating to those closer to you that you are prepared, and desire, to interact on an even level, and that you feel more at peace with your surroundings and relationships.

If you wear this colour and are single, you are communicating to those that can recognise the message your desire to share everything you have with others. You are telling them that you feel a little lonely and want something special in your life.

If you wear this colour on the outer lower body only occasionally, you are less able to express yourself physically or trust others as easily as you may wish. You desire others to see the good you have to offer, but want them to prove their worthiness of it before you show them what you have to give. A white top with a pink skirt or trousers, for example, strengthens the white's powers of 'look but don't touch', whereas a red top with a pink skirt or trousers shows a greater willingness and desire to express your emotions in a physical way.

You should note, though, that if you ignore what the pink wearer has to offer, you will eventually lose them, as their desire when they are wearing pink on the outer lower body is to find an outlet for their emotions of love and compassion. If you fail to notice this, others may take advantage of what you have ignored.

Orange

Orange worn on the lower outer body is a reflection of the wearer's desire to communicate with others, travel, explore and investigate. The logic of yellow has combined with the energy of red and is seeking to find the solution for, or answer to problems, or hardships in the wearer's physical surroundings.

The direction the orange has taken can only be ascertained by the colours worn around it. Orange itself when worn on the outer lower body shows that the mind has become actively involved in expressing the physical direction. The wearer requires both physical and mental stimulation to satisfy their curiosity. The colour shows the wearer's desire to investigate the unknown, come to terms with his environment, and exert more control over the direction of his life.

If you often wear this colour on the outer lower body

you tend to lead rather than be led, ask questions while others remain silent, and frequently question your own actions and decisions.

Peach is a shade of orange that has become diluted with white, and is probably the softest expression of this energy. It can separate itself from the wrongs or rights of other people's lifestyles.

However, the best way to judge the strength of orange is that the stronger the colour, the more physically demonstrative the wearer, while the paler or yellower the orange, the more logical and mental are the controlling forces.

Orange worn on the outer lower body is an indicator that the rebellious side of the wearer's nature is near the surface and about to explode into physical action. If you wear this colour a great deal, you are probably unhappy with your present surroundings or outlets for your mental energy. You may be unorthodox in your views, wanting the world and those around you to adopt your ideals in the hope of a harmonious solution. You are a great communicator of logic, but totally emotional, and fail to see any way forward other than your own. The changes you desire just might benefit everyone, but each should be allowed to accept changes at their own pace and only a few can keep up with the pace of orange.

If you wear this colour only occasionally then you are more mentally assertive, in the direction that you wish your life to go. You have probably been hinting at changes you desire within your environment, and are fed up with others not listening. You want action, not words. Orange is the colour of change, be it good or bad, and people who wear this colour are the bringers of change both to their own environment or the greater environment of the world in which we all live.

Yellow

Yellow garments worn on the outer lower body reflect the logic and thought process under which we put our physical surroundings from time to time. Yellow is the colour of creative logic in its positive context, or cold logic in its negative one. It is a primary colour which reflects from a mustard shade through to the brightest flashes of brilliance.

If you frequently wear yellow on the outer lower body you are the type of person who needs to have a reason for doing what you do. You relate to a bird in the hand rather than two in the bush, and can't understand why people become so emotional when there's a logical solution to most problems.

On the positive side, you are creative, able both to plan, instigate and follow through your ideas and ambitions. On the negative side you expect others to be the efficient machine that you are at times — eating when they are hungry, sleeping only when absolutely necessary, and remaining totally in control of their emotions.

Yellow reflects the higher intellect of man, and when worn on the lower outer area of the body, it never feels totally at home. Yellow wearers never really allow themselves the unrestricted physical freedom of red, pink, white or any of the other colours, and require a reason for doing what they do.

People who wear yellow tend to set themselves a timetable to which they adhere rigidly. Although, they will investigate and open new avenues of exploration, they can become bored and seek other outlets for their creative energies. Yellow wearers tend to be self-critical to extremes, but will snap off the hand of others who criticise them, feeling it is not their place to do so.

If you wear yellow on the outer lower body only occasionally, then your mood is generally more optimistic and sunny. You may feel like a change in the places or haunts you visit, or may just be feeling a little more serious about solutions to certain facets of your lifestyle.

When you wear yellow, you are more likely to be objective to suggestions or situations in your life, wanting to find a hobby or outlet for your physical and mental energy more stimulating or adventurous than that in which you are currently involved.

The negative side of yellow can be viewed as representing destructive or critical mental images either of yourself or those around you which may result in democratic discussions becoming heated arguments, leading to disharmony.

Use the creative energies of this garment colour to plan your future physical environments, rather than force them upon the environments of others around you, and you will achieve the success and reassurance you really desire.

Green

Green trousers and skirts reflect our desire to rest, recuperate and consolidate our physical position.

Green is a neutral colour, combining the warm logic of yellow and the cold emotions of blue. In Nature it is the supporting stem or leaf of the flower which gathers the nutrient energy of the sun for new growth and expansion. Green is worn at a time when we are gathering our energies before the next onslaught. It is the healing colour of nature which allows us to rest in order that we may enter the fray again renewed with energy and vitality.

If you frequently wear green, you have an affinity with Nature, enjoy tranquility and quiet holidays and prefer at times to be left alone with your own thoughts. You are more likely to keep pets or have lots of house plants, live in the country, or become involved with ecology or some wild life charity or concern. You have a natural healing ability and others recognise your ability to take things in your stride.

On the negative side, you may be feeling physically run down and require more help or assistance from others or so you think at the time — but the chore is best done by yourself and you will recoup your strength and do what has to be done.

Green has a calming effect on wearers and they are less likely to be aggressive or physically demonstrative at the times when this type wears green. This does not, however, mean that they are a soft touch. Remember, green consolidates its strength for new growth and expansion, so wearers may be prepared to assist others, but not at the expense of their own patch of land.

If you wear this colour on the lower outer body only occasionally, then you may be feeling tired and run down and require a period of rest or solitude from the stresses of everyday life. It can also be a reflection of the lack of direction into which you put your physical energies, or the feeling that others do not always appreciate the effort that you make on their behalf.

If your partner or associates wear green on this area of the body lend them a hand, give praise where it is due and let up on your own demands for satisfaction for a while. People wearing green need only a short time to recharge their batteries, but can wilt and die without the correct physical encouragement. Wearers of green want to give and share their energies, and need only a little appreciation to show that the effort was worth while. Green is the support colour of Nature between the brown of soil and the colour of the flowers and fertility, and will work silently and ardously for the smallest reward, such as the visitation of the bumble bee, that ensures its fertilisation and rebirth.

Brown

If you wear brown trousers or skirts you are reflecting your physical desire for material security that you can both see and hold in your hand — be it financial or emotional. Brown is the natural bank of soil which contains all the elements for growth not yet born.

If you wear this colour on your outer lower body, you are reflecting a more serious side of your nature which requires financial and material security before you can put your plans, ideals and ambitions into action. The colour is not greedy, it merely requires a degree more material stability than other colours. If you often wear this colour you require those around you to match you deed for deed. You have a lot to offer your environment but do not quite know how to go about giving it. You may be a little bit conservative or stuffy, and slow to adapt to sudden changes in society, prefering the way you know to be tried and tested.

On the positive side, you can be generous and expansive, but on the negative side restrictive feelings that things may not be all they seem can cause hesitation before you commit yourself to projects and ideals. The nutrient chemicals of the soil are there for expansion and you should learn to be more giving, for in return you will also receive all that you have ever dreamed of.

The green shoot which grows from the brown soil becomes a flower and later returns from whence it came. Learn from the lessons of Nature, re-cycle your material wealth and you will achieve all you ever desired. Money can help pass the time, but it cannot bring the real joy of oneness with ourselves.

If you wear this colour only occasionally, then you are reflecting your physical desire to change or consolidate your material position. You may have some bills to pay or just want to be a little more thrifty in order to save for that big occasion or holiday.

Brown simply reflects our desire for stability and security, and within it we plant our roots for future growth and expansion, new directions or creation. It is neither good nor bad, it is only a reflection of how we feel in relation to our overall plan of development. It is not necessarily money-oriented. Some need money to expand and others only love. Brown shows us, when worn on this area of our bodies, that we desire a little more of what makes us feel secure if we are to survive our present circumstances or progress on to others.

Look at the colours "around" the brown in order to ascertain what it is that the wearer requires to satisfy their feelings of security and you'll have the answer to your problems. Brown is a great giver, once it knows that the recipient is a worthy cause.

Purple

Purple when worn on the lower outer physical body is a reflection of our desire to reject the physical environment in which we exist for a more spiritual one.

It is the combination of the physical red and the emotional blue — a warm and cold colour with an inner battle for supremacy over which path to tread. The darker the shade, the more control the emotional blue has, and the more philosophical, spiritual and peaceful are the energies at play. The redder the shade, the more physically demonstrative the energies are. The very pale purples have been strengthened by white which makes them more rigid and old fashioned in their views and outlook.

If you often wear purple on the lower outer body you are more likely to practise meditation, have deep philosophical thoughts, or become involved in orthodox or strange new religions or movements. You may be going through an emotional crisis in one form or another, where whatever decision you make will effect others and you are trying to choose the best path for all. You want to save the world, the whale or whatever has your sympathy, or so you think, whereas in reality you want to harness your own feelings of security. Those who take from life at some time feel they have to give in order to satisfy their own inner feelings of guilt.

If you wear purple on the outer lower body only occasionally, then you are feeling more sympathetic to the needs of others. You are more likely to be pondering the reasons for why you are here, what purpose your present life has or just simply feel more at peace with what you are and what you are doing.

The association of purple with the occult had more to do with its rarity in past centuries than most would think. Anything which was hard to come by was highly prized and used only for special occasions or ceremonies — hence its usage by the church and royalty. With the use of modern dyes and synthetic colourings purple is now used very much more widely and can no longer be associated only with those types of vibrations.

Purple can bring out the more spiritual and peaceful side of ourselves, but with its red content that thought must eventually turn into action, perhaps as reflected in the political intrigue with which the Christian or other religious movements often find themselves involved. So on the lighter side we feel those who wear purple on occasions can be considered more politically active at that time.

Blue

Blue is primarily a colour of emotional healing and regeneration. It has a calming effect upon us which helps us to reorganise and plan our future emotional feelings. When worn on the lower outer body it shows on the positive side that we have recognised our need to react and interact emotionally with others in order to feel more at peace with ourselves. It also indicates that we are making a physical effort to do so.

On the more negative side, it shows the opposite to be so — that we feel emotionally run down and want others to reassure us physically and emotionally that what we are doing is eventually going to be worth while.

If you frequently wear blue on the lower outer body you require a great deal more emotional reassurance in order to feel content and at peace in your surroundings. This must be demonstrated in the physical way your partner makes contact with you and reassures you in your everyday lives. You may feel that others just take you for granted. You do not need them to worship you, but just notice that you are there. On the positive side, it reflects your ability to be physically demonstrative with those same emotions you feel have earned that part of you.

If you wear blue on the outer lower body only occasionally, then it is possible you are feeling emotionally overworked and undernourished at that time. You are in need of spiritual and emotional enlightenment if you are to continue upon your present path.

The calming effect of blue allows you to sit back and reassess your present physical emotional environment — where you stand in it and what you intend to do about it. Blue also has a very sympathetic, caring side to its vibration and many people who wear this colour do so when they have the responsibility or care of others to contend with, such as nurses and social workers.

If you wear blue or feel drawn to blue you are a lot softer than you pretend to be and should learn to express your emotions with more confidence if you are to find the physical security you so ardently desire.

Black

Black is the colour of the hidden and unknown, that which we want to keep to ourselves — our darker sides. Black worn on the lower outer body reflects the wearer's uncertainty as to were they are going to or coming from as regards their ability to control their own destiny. Whether we like it or not, the night hides a host of fears and inhibitions, most of which never actually materialise. It is only the black wearers' fear of being accepted for what they are that inhibits them from attaining what they desire.

If you often wear black clothing on the lower body, you are projecting to others something which you want to be, but are not. It may make you look slimmer than you really are, inject fear into others so they keep out of your way, or hide a host of imaginary phobias from yourself. Black is everything and yet nothing. It fears acceptance and tries to absorb what surrounds it, letting it become a part of itself but failing to give in return, lest it be hurt or not accepted. You are either defensive and secretive about yourself, or a braggart who wants others to accept you on the basis of the fairytales you tell and have come to believe yourself.

On the positive side, black allows its wearer to absorb the knocks we all take from time to time and to arbitrate between disputes of others, as the colour can absorb both views and reflect a balanced answer when there is no personal involvement. Such an existence is seen in the clergy, who remain secretive and withdrawn from the wrongs or rights of other people's lifestyles while being able to give sound advice and spiritual counselling to their congregations. Black is neither good nor bad, pure nor dirty, it merely reflects back what it can absorb.

If you wear this colour only on rare occasions, it is a reflection of your desire to withdraw from the everyday wrongs, rights and responsibilities of your physical lifestyle in order to test the water you are in before you submerge yourself into a final commitment. Black as a colour on the lower body remains on the fence in disputes, dislikes losers, and will bet only on what it thinks is the winning track.

Black is an absorber which takes in everything within its environment, but gives back only what it feels will create the right impression and ensure its own survival. Be nice to black wearers and they will be nice to you, but be nasty to wearers of black at your own peril.

SHIRTS, BLOUSES AND UPPER OUTER BODY ATTIRE

White, pink, red, yellow, green, blue, brown, black, purple.

The colours worn on the upper outer body are indicators of the energy vibrations with which we either feel emotionaly able to cope, or are trying to attract to ourselves. They are indicative of the state of our emotional stability and show the way we wish to be emotionally led.

As in other sections of the manual these colours are read in conjunction with the colours surrounding them or make contact with them. They are, however, a reflection in their own right of the emotional stability of the wearer at the time the colour is being worn. The upper body covers the emotional area of our lives and the outer clothing that which we have consciously recognised and are trying to enact or want to attract to ourselves in order that we may feel emotionally secure. Remember that if you really want an accurate description or understanding of your partner's vibrations, you must learn to mix the physical direction with the emotional feelings to arrive at anything near the right answer. Each item in itself is nothing without the whole being taken into account.

White

White is pure, chaste and without blemish. It wishes to remain so, and when worn on the outer upper body it is indicative of a type who wishes to be seen as an example to all and admired but not touched, as this would make it less than it wishes to be and more than it can perhaps control.

If you wear this colour upper outer garment a lot, other than for work, you feel emotionally cold and unable to trust others with your feelings lest they misuse them. You are very critical of yourself and your own abilities or inabilities, but tolerate no advice from others. Inside you are an emotional turmoil wanting to live, give and share all that you have, but fearing where it may lead you. This makes you test those around you until they become fed up with your possessive ways and wander on elsewhere. This only leads you to the conclusion that you were right in the first place and make it even more difficult for you to trust someone else the next time around.

On the positive side you have a feeling of grandeur, are able to command emotionally all your resources and stand back from the wrongs or rights of the world, even if it means becoming like a robotic android who operates only on pure logic without feelings, and cannot understand why other people act so emotionally at times.

White needs to separate itself from other colours lest it become involved in other people's problems. It has no time for this, as it can barely control its own, let alone be responsible for other people's. If you wear this colour on the upper outer body you can at times be as cold as the snow on the iciest mountain peak. That's a shame, for white energy has all at its command if it only put it to use. Learn to trust others more with all your feelings. It may help you to lighten your self-imposed burden.

If you wear white on the upper outer body only on infrequent occasions, it is a reflection of your desire to disassociate yourself from the wrongs or rights of an emotional part of your life, like stepping into the shower to rid yourself of a summer's day perspiration. It is indicative of your desire to remove yourself from areas of your life where you feel no blame for what has gone wrong. White wearers on this area of the body have problems of their own to sort out and don't want to become involved in the wrongs or rights of other people. It is an indicator of a period of self denial or a profound announcement of your innonence or involvement in what is occuring in your social circle.

Pink

Pink worn on the upper outer body can have only two reasons for being there; either as an expression of the emotional peace and contentment the wearer feels that period of his emotional life is going through, or as an expression of the emotional warmth and compassion he has to offer should someone but recognise this and interact with them.

Even in its negative context, pink worn on the emotional area of the body, has a warmth and desire to share beyond the average, and if it is recognised and used, then it cannot be negative.

If you often wear pink on the upper outer body, you are expressing your feelings of emotional contentment and stability. The emotional side of your life is at that time all you desire, and you have an extra warmth and compassion to give those you love. You feel the desire to share with others the happiness and peace that you feel, and are apt to be more demonstrative both physically and emotionally at this time.

If you wear pink only occasionally, then you need to clear your life of any problems or inhibitions before you can express your feelings of contentment. Your relationships tend to be of a more up-and-down nature, and you wear the pink on the more peaceful cycles. You need to learn to communicate more of your inner desires to your chosen mate, so that the feelings of pink can be brought to the surface.

Red

Red garments worn on the upper outer body are indicative of the high level of physical, emotional energy which the wearer may be experiencing. This is not one of the best places to wear red, as it can cause the heart to rule the head, and bring unnecessary conflict into the wearer's life. The emotional area of the upper outer body does not like to be rushed, or pushed into making decisions, and red energy worn here can do just that.

If you often wear red on the upper outer body, you take life at a fast pace, have little time for long-term emotional commitments and would prefer to be doing what you feel you enjoy, without realising it may not suit your associates. You need positive and demonstrative reactions to your emotional needs and desires, but never sit still for long enough to appreciate what you actually have. You can flit from partner to partner, or party to party, at the drop of a hat, always seeking the unknown and adventurous, but never quite content with what you have. There may be something better around the next corner! You show your feelings to extremes of love and hate, but find it hard to maintain a balance between the two. You can be very possessive of what you consider to be yours, even if it may not actually be your own.

You are emotionally assertive, for only when you feel in control do you feel at ease. Yet it is this desire to meet your equal that makes you drive others so hard. You must learn to soften your approach or you will find your relationships, though great at the stant are shortlived and leave you with a feeling of emptiness which you admit only to yourself.

If you wear this colour only occasionally, then you are reflecting your desire to be more emotionally active and assertive. You know the direction in which you wish to express your emotional energy but have not yet found an outlet for it. You may find yourself desiring to go out more, become more socially active or just spend more time with someone you love.

Red is the colour of energy and when worn on the emotional area of the body the emotional energy is high. Red energy can be very creative or self-destructive, but whatever use it is put to, once set in motion it is the hardest energy to halt or control.

So next time your wear red, remember you may be feeling charged, happy and content, but this energy can turn 180 degrees and create those emotional situations which we regret when we have the time to ponder upon them. However by then, the damage has already been done.

Yellow

Yellow garments worn on the outer upper body are reflections of the desire to bring your emotional feelings under some measure of control. Yellow is the colour of intellect and logic and those who wear this colour on the emotional area of the body tend to need a logical reason for doing what they do, or being where they are. When you wear yellow on this area of the body, you are apt to be less responsive to other people's emotional needs, being too concerned with what direction you require your own emotions to take. You are apt to be overly critical of others and what you consider to be the wrongs or rights of their lifestyle.

If you often wear this colour on the upper outer body

you are looking for a solution or reason for your emotional feelings. You may find yourself becoming less involved in one relationship or looking for a way to improve what you have. You can be very picky with those close to you and are apt to be critical of both yourself and those around you at this time.

Yellow can be very creative and it is this sunnier vibration of the colour that is its saviour on this part of the body. Yellow wearers want, need and demand some form of change in their emotional understanding of those who are important to them.

When you wear the colour yellow, you may be seeking to bring to the light emotional parts of yourself that you have either failed to face up to in the past and are trying to do now. Or you may be critical of those around you for not understanding what you feel you should be getting from your relationships. Yellow wearers react better in intellectual relationships than the physical ones.

If you wear yellow only occasionally, then you are trying to bring to the fore part of your emotional feelings that you feel is being neglected. You want those around you to listen to you and not just take you for granted or treat you as a piece of the household furniture. It is a momentary desire to bring back into line your emotional relationships, which should mean that, for the majority of the time, you are content with how others react with you in those relationships. Wearers of yellow have a view to put, and as long as that view is listened to, they are prepared to go along with its logical conclusion.

The negative use of yellow can be a dictorial approach to emotional relationships which would eventually doom them to failure. Dictators have tried throughout history to impose their will upon others. Whether they were right or wrong in their belief does not matter, because all dictators eventually fall to a revolt.

Green

Green is the neutral healing colour of the human aura and, when worn on the upper outer emotional part of the body, it expressess the wearer's desire or need for a rest from the stresses and demands that those close to him have made upon him. Green is also a colour of growth and expansion when it has collected its reserves for new growth, so the two opposites can be at play when this colour is worn. One side is the renewal and regeneration of emotional stability which requires to rest and be tended. The other is the expansion of fertile new shoots that can spring into growth once the energy reserves of nature have been gathered and put to use.

If you frequently wear this colour, you may find that you are constantly drained emotionally by those around you. You may have a large family to care for, a sick relative to look after or may just be feeling a bit under power and need a course of vitamins to pick yourself up. Green wearers have a deeply sympathetic side to their nature which leads them into jobs or circum-stances which leave them with the responsibilities of others in one way or another. They tend to have a feel for Nature and wildlife and can be avid gardeners or have lots of house plants.

Continually caring for others does, however, leave green wearers with a hole in their lives, as this ability means they sometimes fail to find anyone to care for them. If you wear negative green you can be too lazy to get up and do the things you want to, and end up blaming those close to you for your own shortcomings. The overall effect of green, when worn a lot by individ-uals, indicates one who gives emotionally to many rather than one, someone who works for society rather for themselves.

If you wear this colour on the upper outer body only occasionally, then you wear it at a time when you are feeling emotionally and physically drained. You have put or are still putting, a great deal of emotion into a project or relationship, but are taking a breather to recuperate your own energy reserves. Green has very strong healing and regenerative vibrations, and those who wear this colour are usually recuperating after periods of hard work, emotional stress or physical activity. The darker the green, the stronger the need to rest becomes. The lighter the shade, the quicker the recovery of the energy will be. Some say green is a cold colour, but in my opinion nothing could be further from the truth, for without the regenerative healing of green, the world we live in would grind to a halt.

Blue

When you wear the colour blue on the upper outer of the body, you are wearing the colour of emotional feelings on an emotional area of the body. It is with this in mind that we state that the two following effects will take place; either the blue worn on the concious area will allow you to take control of and express your emotional requirements openly, or it will indicate that you are at an emotional low and require others to assist you with or lighten your emotional load.

The other indicator of the blue energy in play is the shade. The darker the shade, the more the wearer would appear to be trying to restrict the emotional energy because of either insecurity or a lack of confidence. The lighter the shade, the more the emotional energy would appear to be directed towards the help or emotional support of others.

This is not an absolute rule, and, as with other colours, the surrounding vibrations must also be taken into account.

If you often wear blue on the upper outer body you can be mistrustful of other people's motives or response to you in personal relationships.

You require a degree of reassurance before you commit yourself fully, though you have a sympathetic ear for any one in need. You could be a good arbitrator in other people's problems, but for some reason find it difficult to maintain a stable relationship with others. You can be over-demonstrative of your emotions, perhaps even to the point of scaring others away with the intensity of commitment that you desire from them. Once you do eventually find what you are seeking, you can be most loyal and faithful, but you do expect as good as you give. Blue wearers tend to chatter to hide a degree of shyness that is their inherent birth-right.

If you wear blue on the upper outer body only occasionally, then you are indicating that you could be going through a period of emotional stress, or feel emotionally run down and need a rest. Blue is the colour of emotional regeneration or healing and it is worn when we need reassurance, sympathy or just feel run down and want a rest.

The positive side of blue worn on this part of the body is an expression of our emotional control over ourselves and the ability to use our spare energy to help others with their problems. Blue emotional energy can be either restrictive and inhibiting, or creative and expansive, — the choice is yours to make.

Brown

Brown is the colour of wealth, reserves of physical energy and the bank of Nature. When worn on the upper outer body it reflects the wearer's need for independence and material security. The positive aspects of brown on this body area are generosity, material support and the ability to share the emotional worries of others. (Blue water feeds brown earth.) The negative aspects of brown are the excessive desire for material possessions in order to feel emotionally secure. Brown in its darker shades reflects the deeper needs of the colour, be they positive or negative, while the paler shades can be indicative of those who try to rid themselves of the material preconditioning within which we all learn to exist.

If you frequently wear this colour on the upper outer body, you need to keep your own source of income or finances in emotional relationships. You do not like to be held to emotional ransom by others, and will always want to pay your way no matter how lazy or inactive you may sometimes feel. You can be generous with those you feel deserve what you have to offer, but can be just as mean with those you feel do not. You can be very much a loner for long periods, then out every night of the week to make up for lost time.

Once you find the person you feel is right for you, there is nothing you would not give them or do for them if it is within your power. You must, however, be able to justify your actions to yourself and can lean towards the logical yellow at times.

If you wear brown only occasionally on the upper outer body, you may be feeling financially flush and want to hit the town and share with others your feelings of emotional security. Alternatively, the opposite effect may cause you to stay in, as you feel worried about your monetary situation and would rather stay in and save what you have, perhaps to pay a bill, which has probably not even arrived, but which you feel may be substantial. Brown wearers tend to be at one extreme or another — either at ease or at odds with themselves or those around them. The real root cause of any problems they encounter, however, is the desire for material security before they can really relax and enjoy their emotional lives to the full.

Black

Black is a colour of hidden secrets, mystery and even fear. When worn on the outer upper body, it is a reflection of the wearer's inability to interact with others without first testing the ground they are about to tread. Black wearers of this garment type lack a degree of confidence, as they wear a colour which absorbs whatever is around it before reflecting anything back.

The secretive side of black needs to see what those within its environment finds acceptable before it decides whether it is what they are looking for. It is hardly surprising that it is known as a colour of mystery, as without communicating why, it can just disappear without reason from the environment in its search for emotional fulfilment. Black wearers need to test the emotional water of their chosen environment before they can commit themselves or feel secure in that environment. They tend to take rather than give on an emotional level, and can be likened to sponges absorbing all that is offered, be it good or bad, but needing a bit of a squeeze to give anything in return.

I am not trying to imply that this is a bad colour for it is not. It is just that little less able to respond on an emotional level than most other colours, and gives only under pressure.

If you wear a lot of black on the upper outer body you need to open up more to others. You seem to become what you feel your environment demands of you, rather than expressing what you would really like to be. You can be very secretive about your past or personal relationships, and at times are, or appear to be, in a world all your own.

Black is neither good nor bad, it merely has the ability to hide both actions within itself, so if you wear a lot of black, understand and respect yourself and your views more, project your confidence in matters that you feel are important to you and you will rediscover your lost self-respect.

If you wear this colour on the outer upper body only occasionally, then you are withdrawing from the stresses of maintaining emotional relationships. You may be having a secret love affair which you wish to hide from others, or perhaps just do not want to be the leader any more and want someone else to take responsibility for your emotional direction.

Black's positive side also allows us to hide facets of our emotions from those close to us. But, like it or not, black absorbs and has something to hide, and although some may think that is bad, many a masterpiece has been left undiscovered in a darkened room and had to be brought out into the light for others to admire for what it really was.

Purple

People who wear the colour purple on the upper outer body are the optimists of life, always there with a helping hand when others need it, kind, considerate and openly demonstrative of their emotions. Purple is the colour of spirituality though its negative side on this emotional area of the body is to be a little old fashioned, stuck in a time and era far moved from present realities. Purple can be worn when we philosophise on the higher vibrations of our lifestyles: 'Why are we here?', 'Why do I do as I do?' Who knows what thoughts pass through the minds of others? Purple needs to know why people act as they do and justify it in the great scale of things.

If you often wear this colour on the upper outer body, you would make a great preacher or famine relief agent, as you have the emotional drive to improve both spiritually and physically the conditions we must all live in. You can, however, try to impose your views on those that fail to listen, like the evangelist preacher who stands outside the public house on Saturday nights warning us of the sins of the flesh. Purple wants to help others, for in so doing it satisfies its own emotional feelings of being wanted and needed.

If you wear the colour purple only occasionally on the upper emotional part of the body, it could be that you disapprove of the actions of someone close to you, or of how you feel they treat you emotionally. You could be at an emotionally critical phase on your bio-chart, or just desire to separate yourself from the wrongs or rights of your situation.

On the positive side, you have a deep need to communicate a caring side of your nature to those close to you, but may need them to recognise what you are trying to say. Purple, on this part of the body, tends to be more mental than physical so if you find yourself pondering on the reason for our existence and then remember that you are wearing purple, you will have at least solved one of your emotional puzzles.

UNDERWEAR

**White, pink, red, yellow, orange, green, blue,
brown, black, purple.**

Do not read this section if you are embarrased by
concepts of sexuality, be they orthodox or a little more
unusual than the general majority.

It is difficult to know where to begin in this section,
for who can comprehend what we keep hidden. Underwear is the garment closest to the skin, it is both our last
garment of physical protection as well as that which
covers our self-created emotional embarrassment. It is a
combination of our physical and emotional selves, reflecting our innermost secrets, inhibitions, hidden ta-
lents and the way we relate to the world in which we
live. Only those closest to us are privileged to stand in
its light, and only then after hard-won trust.

In some cases, underwear is not worn at all. This is
self-explanatory as it shows clearly that the person has
felt restricted by the society and environment in which
they have been conditioned to live. Even though they
conform to that society, their bodies rebel in an act of
freedom which they feel unable to express in their
normal surroundings.

Those who wear no underwear need a degree of
personal freedom that is also reflected in their love
lives. They do not like to be tied to boring routines, but
although they may pretend to be total freedom seekers,
this is not the case. Variety is the spice of life, and if
they can find that with one partner, then they will.
However, this is rarely the case. Those that wear no
underwear can be in too much of a rush, wanting to do

too many things in too short a time, or spreading their energies thinly on the ground and so eventually wearing down their resolve. They need a firm base to operate from, and it is this which inhibits their desire for total freedom.

If you wear no underwear, you have a deep need to be accepted by others but fail to communicate this. Try to break free and create that safe world of your own as far away from emotional responsibilities as you can. Here today and gone tommorrow could be a good adage for this type. You need to be able to break free from restrictive emotional relationships without feeling any guilt or responsibility for your actions or the need to explain to others why you felt it necessary to do so.

White
If you wear a lot of white on the inner upper and lower body area then you are more of a conformist than most. You have deep-rooted beliefs and ideals which were probably implanted in your early childhood and can lead you into being a little old fashioned. The purity of white on this body area can be an indicator that you are at heart very honest and trustworthy, sticking both to your morals and the tried and tested routines with which you find a real sense of security.

People who wear white can branch out into any colour of the spectrum if they so desire but needs to be admired and respected before they feel any real degree of acceptance in emotional and physical relationships.

On the negative side, wearers can be highly critical of the moral behaviour of those around them, believing that such actions should be confined to the privacy of one's own home. They can be very businesslike in public, reserving their affections and emotions for their private lives. It is difficult to get them to try something new as it may not conform to what they feel is right and proper. People who wear white all the time can be sexually inactive or even frigid, though this is not a hard and fast rule. They are the couples who may link arms in public but would shun a close embrace in case others think them to be what they are not.

If you wear this colour only occasionally on the inner upper and lower body, then you may be going through a period of physical or emotional inactivity. You may feel others have been using you, or that they have put excessive demands on you which you are assessing before you either reject them or accept them, dependent upon your own early emotional and physical preconditioning of what is considered right or wrong.

White's positive side can appear cold and barren as it may totally reject physical advances, believing that it could soil a part of themselves with which they have never been able to feel comfortable. White is a colour which reflects, in its positive mode, purity of thought and action. It can be quite old fashioned and restrictive in its views and physical expression, and will need to feel what it does is accepted by the general majority as being correct and proper if it is to fulfil itself. If the wearers of white meet a partner who can convince them that what they desire is so, then they will put 100 per cent effort into all they do, being of a view that if a job's worth doing then it's worth doing properly. White underwear wearers are also likely to be more loyal than those who favour other colours unless they feel that their mate makes what they consider to be unhealthy demands upon them. White can become or reflect any colour of the spectrum and has the ability to be whatever the wearer desires, should they ever gain the confidence to use what they have.

Pink

If you wear pink underwear you have a mixture of both the purity of white and the energetic pleasure of red. You are warm and compassionate and are prepared to try most things at least once if it helps your relationship to improve, but only with the one you love and not a second time if you found the act offends your own nature. Pink's vibrations are the colour of the physical and emotional joining as one in an expression of relaxation and contentment. Pink underwear wearers can derive as much pleasure from a sexual act as they feel their partner does. However, they will venture on to find someone else if they do not have that receptivity from their chosen mate, as they require their joining to be a complete thing which is pleasurable to both. They are more likely to give before they take and have an inner desire to share with someone special all they have. They are romantics at heart, believing in true love, and can be demonstrative of their emotional and physical feeling in public, wanting to show off their enjoyment of fulfilled love. If you see a couple in a deep embrace on a railway station, barely able to let go as the train pulls out, you could assume that one of them wears pink underwear. Pink is a warm colour of both emotional and physical love which we should all strive to obtain in our lifetime.

If you wear pink underwear only occasionally, you desire to find and fulfil the love you have always dreamed of, but feel unable to maintain this degree of trust for long periods. At the time of wearing the garment, your desire to be closer to someone emotionally is at a stronger level. You are more receptive to the advances of others if you have not yet found what you seek. Or you may want to share with others your feelings of joy and happiness at that time. The inner body is — we must remember — our inner selves and only we can demonstrate these feelings to those around us if we are to find what we desire.

Pink on this part of the body shows that we have both the desire and ability to fulfil our wildest dreams with someone we think special in our lives. We must, however, still learn to show our feelings to others. Otherwise they will not be recognised and fulfilled, which would deny joy and happiness to both parties. Keep the colour locked within and dreams may be all that you ever have.

Pink can have no real negative side effects other than its own inability to express what it so often feels. Use your ability to love, care and share, in the same way as you would want others to treat you, and you will achieve all the joy and happiness of your dreams.

Red

Red is assertive, energetic and forceful. It knows what it wants, and usually gets it. Otherwise it moves on to more stimulating climes. When worn as underwear, the wearer is expressing a need to be physically assertive and in control of his or her inner self. This can show in two ways. The wearer may be the silent type you can't quite fathom. Others seem to obey their subtle body language without knowing why. You know instinctively that their anger would be unbearable, so you never push them that far. They blend into an environment and take in all that is going on around them. Before you realise it, you find yourself under the sway of their power. This type tends to wear lots of white or black as outer clothing to help them on their path to self-satisfaction and security. They can give a great feeling of security and protection to those they take under their wing, but are very possessive of what they consider to be theirs.

The other type of red underwear wearers are just the opposite. They blatantly express what they want to do, can be coarse or aggressive both in how they express themselves and how they treat those around them. If they fail to find what they are looking for in one environment, they will move on to another in search of their dreams. This type tends to wear yellows and blues as outer clothing.

If you wear red underwear only occasionally, then you have a positive feeling of security which you wish to communicate to those close to you. You are readily able to interact physically with those around you, and desire some form of outlet for your emotional and physical feelings.

On the positive side, you feel more confident, adventurous and assertive; able both to communicate your desires and enact them in the company you have chosen. You may change your routine meeting places or social circles at this time, wanting to experience something new and invigorating.

On the negative side, you are fed up with your current social and physical environment, desiring or demanding some form of change in how you feel others see you or treat you. You may feel that those who should be seeing what you have to offer, are not doing so and you are ready to launch a storm of protest if they do not take notice soon.

Red is at its most destructive on this area of the body, as it is self-destructive. In demanding attention from others too forcefully, you may drive them away and lose what you felt you wanted. Once committed to one path, the energy of the wearer is hard to turn aside.

Either because they are too stubborn, or too full of foolish pride, these people cannot blame themselves for problems, or make the first move towards a peaceful solution.

When you assess red, think of it in terms of human blood. Healthy oxygenated blood is a bright scarlet, regenerating the vital cells of the body. Spent blood, on the other hand, is darker and in need of recycling.

Yellow

Yellow is neither a popular nor common colour for underwear and this is hardly surprising as few people are capable of being totally logical and unemotional. If you do wear this colour a lot, then you must have been seriously affected by the circumstances of your early emotional conditioning, for you are unable to express or communicate your emotions and must feel either very lonely or at odds with the majority of people for the greater part of your existence.

Yellow can be a creative logic, but in this area of the body it is out of place, born beyond its time with ideals or views that do not conform, or will not be tolerated by the general populus. Yellow on this area of the body means that the wearer has become a machine rather than an individual, requiring both a logical reason for his or her own existence and for doing, giving or inter-acting with others. This type can become very cold and dictatorial as they must always have an ulterior motive for their actions and feel themselves to be the originator and controller of their own circumstances. The sun may be the core of our solar system, but it alone dictates whether we have growth or dissolution in our sur-roundings.

Yellow can be a warm giver of life, but when worn on this part of the body it requires that others recognise what it has given and show respect or homage for its generosity.

When worn only occasionally, the yellow energy has taken control of the physical and emotional body to create something new and stimulating in your life. It has allowed you to look at both yourself and those around you with a cold, critical eye, in order that you may regenerate or find your path if you have strayed from it. You are liable to be more self-critical at this time and may withdraw from commitments while you assess what you have to offer and whether to continue on that particular path.

Don't go around thinking yellow is a totalitarian energy, self-destructive and unfeeling, as this is not the case. The sun sets each evening and allows the Earth below to rest before it rises the next morning so that the world may yet again grow and flourish. Yet even as it gives, the sun reminds us that without it we would be nothing. Man needs a sense of direction in order to expand his horizons and grow beyond himself, and it is the positive side of yellow that allows him this expansion.

Orange

Orange is another colour for underwear which does not quite vibrate to the correct energies for this part of the body. It is the colour of both a thinker and a doer, though someone who tends to jump in feet first, and allow the heart to rule the head. The combination of logical yellow and energetic red can give us purpose and help us achieve our dreams, but Man is far less able to keep up with the energies of orange than he may think.

Uranium and atomic power vibrate to this energy, and though it can be put to constructive and beneficial use in its positive sense, its negative uncontrollable side is the mass destructive energy of the nuclear bomb. If you wear this colour a lot, you may liken yourself to the type who has all or nothing, who is either hyperactive — a go-getter — or inactive, mentally burnt out, tired, self-destructive to extremes. Orange energy tends to fluctuate between the two extremes — either the giver of great gifts, or the destroyer of all it has and all around it.

Orange underwear wearers need to have a tremendous degree of self control if they are to learn to live with the power of the gods. When used on its positive side this energy has no obstacle that it cannot surmount, and no task which it feels unable to accomplish.

Green

When we wear the colour green as a colour which reflects our combined physical and emotional selves, we are expressing our neutrality and ability to help and assist others. Green is a colour of rest, regeneration and physical healing. If you wear this colour underwear a lot, then on the positive side you are able to assist, comfort and help others, being able to give of yourself unstintingly for the betterment of those around you.

You have a peaceful approach to everyday problems and are more likely to be able to give rather than to take, for in so doing you find the inner peace that you seek. Green energy can make you an excellent arbitrator in other people's conflicts. Your tastes are more likely to be simple, and you may be a conservationist, ecologist or become involved with what you consider to be worthy causes. You should feel at home with Nature and would find more contentment at home than out at one of the local nightspots. Since the energy of green is orientated to give rather than to take, you must ensure that you do not allow others to take advantage of your generosity.

When you wear negative green, the need is to absorb the energies around you in order to feel safe and secure yourself. You can be a depressive, always fearing the worst is going to happen, and this stops you enjoying what you really have.

If you wear green only occasionally, you may, on the positive side, feel a little more charitable with your feelings and emotions. You may desire to become more involved in projects or ideals in your surroundings, or find yourself the shoulder that other people come to cry on. Negative green feels physically inactive. Its energy is dissipated and spent, and it requires the energy of the sun and a period of rest and inactivity in order to recharge its batteries. It wants others to return what it feels it has given to them so that it may again enter the fray with renewed energy and vigour to accomplish the tasks at hand.

Green energy requires more foreplay and reassurance in order to contribute to a worthy cause or partner. Once it has been convinced of this, it gives its all and expects the same in return. Green energy does not like to be rushed into making decisions and would rather be left to make them at its own pace.

Wearers of this energy are the nurses, workers in charitable institutions, farmers or famine relief agents of this world. They feel that by improving the surroundings of others they also increase their own chances of survival, though this is not a conscious aspect of green.

Green on the negative can be very envious of what others have and the adage 'green with envy' was not born from nothing.

Blue

Blue underwear is, after white and pink, the most popular colour for women in this garment type. This is hardly surprising in today's society. Blue's positive energy protects the emotional self from the knocks of everyday life. It has healing and regenerative emotional energy which most of us feel the need to draw upon in this ever-competetive world.

If you often wear blue underwear, you may find it increasingly difficult to cope with the emotional pressures and limitations that society lumps upon you. You can be emotionally defensive, fearing to trust others lest they disrespect or misuse that trust. The darker the blue, the less you are able to give emotionally unless you feel really able to trust those you are with. The lighter the shade, the more able you are to share your emotional insecurities and strengths with others in the hope of finding eventual happiness and contentment.

This colour on the inner physical and emotional area of the body can cause people to lack confidence in themselves, which in turn leads them to require more reassurance than most. Positive blue energy has a sympathetic ear for a friend in need, and will remain a life-long friend with those it trusts, but takes time to feel totally at ease — if, indeed, it ever does.

If you wear blue underwear only occasionally, then when you wear it you may feel the need for reassurance that your chosen path, partner or career is worth while and of use to both yourself and those around you. Or you may feel that you have a period of emotional contentment with both body and soul, and wish to share with others the joy which you feel all could experience if only they understood how.

To be physically and emotionally demonstrative of its emotions when feeling stable and with the ability to share feelings of contentment with loved ones is the positive application of blue energy. The negative outlets are not outlets at all, rather frustrations which the wearer feels. For either they lack the ability to trust others with all of themselves, or they blame others for their own lack of emotional security. Blue can be an indicator of a period of stress to come, a warning of a form of emotional starvation which is expressed in the saying, 'He went a funny shade of blue before he collapsed with a heart attack'. In this case, however, the sickness and attack is directed at a relationship rather than at a bodily organ. Just as a blue colour can indicate a poor circulation in the physical body, so can it indicate a lack of direction in the spiritual.

Brown

Brown underwear reflects the wearer's need for material security from threat of attack fron any source before the body and spirit can operate as one. Brown is a colour, on the positive side, of hidden resources, wealth and stability. It allows the roots of others to grow into it and use it as a stable base, while at the same time it uses them to ensure that unwanted erosion does not take place without its consent. Brown energy can be either very giving or very mean, it can help you to grow if it feels you worthy, or stunt your growth. Just as in nature, brown is a mixture of rocky, barren soil, nutricious peaty ground or arid, dry sand. Only a foolish farmer would plant the wrong crop into the wrong type of soil.

If you often wear brown underwear, you must have material success in your own environment before you can justify giving to the growth and expansion of others. You need to prove to yourself your ability to succeed before you can unwind, relax and begin to enjoy life to its full with someone you care for. You can fluctuate between great generosity and meaness, dependent upon your own feelings of stability. You desire to impress others and be admired for what you have achieved, and will be able to relate only to those who understand your deeply hidden, though sensitive nature.

Brown has a lot to offer both to those close to it and the world as a whole. But it must create its own stable base to operate from before it feels able to interact on a physical level. Brown is very expansive and needs to be treated as it treats others if it is to meet its true match in life. Brown gives nutrients to green which flower and return to brown. This is both Nature's way and the brown wearer's way of saying, 'I am prepared to give you what you need to survive, if you are prepared to give me the same in whatever may be necessary.'

If you wear brown only occasionally, you are reflecting a need to consolidate your material position in order to enter a new period of growth. Your bills may be due in the near future — whether they be emotional, sexual or financial — and you are preparing either to give what is due to others, or take what is due to you. Brown could be considered the womb of the world where all things are seeds awaiting that spark of light which will give them the message that it is now safe to grow and expand upon their chosen path.

Black

Now we have arrived at the final conflict, the least understood and least expressive of all the colours which can be worn on the inner body as underwear. Black has its meanings corrupted by the sensual seekers of self-gratification who use its energy to hide their own feelings of insecurity and instability. They do so in order to create a temporary environment of mystery and excitement in which they can hide away from the realities of the true expression of themselves, even to the extent of believing they are more than they ever could be. Black is at its most negative and corrupt when worn on this part of the body as it creates a false environment both in the wearer and those they associate with. It may outwardly make you appear sexier or more confident with others, but unless you learn to like yourself for what you are, you will never find what you truly seek, merely a diversion from the realities of your life.

If you often wear black underwear, you lack confidence both in yourself as a caring individual and in your ability to be a part of a complete relationship. You are more worried about how you feel others see you, and try to create a false environment in which you think others will care more for you.

Black absorbs all that comes its way like a sponge, but needs to be squeezed if it is to give to others what they desire. Positive black energy can maintain an equilibrium in relationships, but it is my contention that it is a false sense of security that must be faced up to and conquered if the wearer is to find what they really seek.

If you wear black underwear only for those special occasions with someone you love, then relate to it as an indicator of your willingness to become what your partner desires, so that both of you can be satisfied. It is associated with sexier times and freedom from inhibitions, and it is this use of black energy which allows you to become, for a time, more extrovert than you would normally be in public. Use it for what it is, rather than let it use you, making you both a slave to your own inhibitions and those of others.

Black is not a bad colour energy, only a misused one. It is your responsibility whether you see it to deceive yourself and those around you, or merely as a temporary shield while you gather your resources to enter the fray anew. Black can give you the chance to test the water without getting too wet, but be careful it does not pull you in beyond your depth, as it has many hidden dangers. If you had a large belly and wore black to make yourself appear slimmer, the illusion only lasts as long as you wear the garment. You must eventually face up to the fact of its existence and either learn to live with it or put yourself on a diet and get rid of it.

Purple

Purple is the colour of the higher mind of Man, his spiritual energy source and his higher thought vibrations, such as the ability to philosophise. When this colour is worn on the inner self area of the body, the wearer is expressing their desire to reach beyond the material preconditioning of their environment in the search for completeness and attainment.

Purple is a mixture of emotional blue and physical red, which can be a bad combination if the negative red should ever overpower the blue. When you judge this colour you must remember that the constructive energy is to elevate the self above the greeds and wrongs of the material world, and to seek a life free from strife, challenge, or the wrongs or rights of immediate surroundings. Its negative application can be sexual misuse and gratification, the desire for worldly power and wealth, as seen in some religious movements and their higher orders in centuries gone by.

If you wear a lot of this colour, you have the type of inner self which desires to save the world from itself. You seek through your own thought processes the answer to the mysteries that surround you, be they material or spiritual. You need to feel at one with something, but you have not yet fully discovered what that something is.

Purple energy is hard to define on its own, but finds its expression or direction for its energy in the colours that surround it. It does need to be alone to ponder its direction, but not all the time, as it has a deep-seated need to communicate its answers and solutions to someone it feels will put them to use. Purple energy is the energy of mental rather than physical action. Its wearers need a partner who is both mentally and physically stimulating. They are likely to object to great wealth for individuals, feeling that all should have a share in life's fortunes and strifes. They are a secretive bunch, and although you may have had them in your house for years you will never fully understand the source of their often contradictory ideals.

Negative purple energy has allowed the frustration of not being able to find what he seeks, drown his sorrow in that which he can feel, taste and touch. It may covet what belongs to others, always hoping to find its direction one day. Yet, it succeeds only in burying itself in the seedier side of life. Purple energy was given so that Man may eventually aspire to greater and more spiritual realms. Few can fully control its direction.

If you wear this colour underwear only on occasions, then you are reflecting your inner desire to separate yourself from some form of inner spiritual conflict. You may have a degree more understanding of other people's emotions, but will require them to recognise the fact that you want peace and not strife in your life and that they had better sort themselves out quickly before you lose your patience with them. Purple can be a lonely colour as it chooses its own inner path which few others can truly comprehend.

ACCESSORIES

Accessories such as belts, jewellery, women's make-up, scarves, ties and so on, have no real energy of their own. They are a beacon or indicator of energy that the wearer wishes to highlight or bring to the attention of others.

The belt or head scarf could be considered separately. The belt acts as bridge between the emotional upper body and the physical lower body, while the hat or head scarf is indicative of our mental state of awareness. It is not necessary however, to give them a chapter of their own. You can simply look up the colour in relation to the area of the body it highlights, and apply the energy to the colour worn there.

Eyeliner on a woman is a reflection of how she emotionally sees herself, while the scarf around the neck indicates her ability to communicate her insecurities (throat).

The jewels on her hands may distract you from facets of her, or attract you to parts of her. Gold and silver are not classed as colours in this manual, though gold is a reflection of a deep yellow or rich brown and could be considered a material indicator, while silver is a higher form of white or a rich grey and could be considered to be more emotional. The same applies to other metals and minerals. Both gold and silver operate as energies on a dimension beyond this one and few would actually be aware of how to put those energies to their higher use.

TYPES AND DESIGNS OF CLOTHING

When assessing what your subject is wearing you can also tell their type of mood or direction by the texture and design of the clothes. The following pointers will help you in this assessment.

Fabrics

Coarse, woven material is worn at a time when the subject is either more protective of their surroundings or wishes to shield themselves from harm.

Smooth, silky or satiny material is worn when the subject wants to draw attention to a specific colour vibration or area. This could cause problems if they keep smoothing the material, or they could be very comfortable with it if they do not.

Animal skins, furs and the like are indicators of a degree of animal instinct that the wearer may apply in overcoming their problems. Leather can be a hunter, while fur prefers to be hunted, but it depends on the type of fur which is worn. A lion skin could have a tiger within.

Linens, cottons and the like are worn more by the practical, down-to-earth types who both want to be warm and cool depending upon the surroundings and circumstances.

Synthetic clothing is worn by those that are in a hurry. The stay-press materials or easier cuts allow this type to be what they want, when they want.

All patterns and designs indicate how the wearer expresses the colour energy at play and how they put it to constructive or destructive use.

Stripes worn running down the body are indicative of prison bars, and restrict a part of the subject's expression. They have something to lock up and hide away, be it a degree of fat that the bars detract from, or the colour vibration itself.

Stripes worn across the body are indicators of the subject allowing that energy to peek through, as in lifting one slat of a venetian blind to see what is on the other side.

Grids and grills worn in clothing indicate that the wearer feels restricted and frustrated in their desire to express colour energy. They feel frustrated that they do not have any degree of success, or that they restrict others.

Plain clothing shows that the colour energy worn is at a stronger level and must find expression.

Floral designs can relate to the flowers worn. An open rose can express love, but not in blue. A closed rose with thorns may say, 'Look, but if you touch you'll get pricked'. Try to relate the design to the colour.

Boxes are expressions of the wearer's desire for more security in their lives.

Triangles indicate ambition and energy, the direction of which is indicated by where the triangle points. Upwards is directed energy, to the side dissipated energy, and downwards self-destructive energy.

TWO CASES OF INTERPRETATION.

Case One.

Subject Female
Age 22

Colours Worn
The subject was wearing a soft pink T-Shirt with a white belt and a white skirt. She wore no stockings or socks and had on a medium-heeled pair of red pointed shoes. Her underwear was pale blue and she was wearing only a little eye liner and pink lipstick with a band of white beads around her neck.

The Interpretation
The soft pink top shows that the wearer is emotionally responsive to others. She either has a degree of emotional security, or actively seeks to show others her emotional ability to share what she has to offer.

The white belt and skirt reflect her feelings of physical insecurity. She is chaste and pure in the wider sense, desires only one faithful partner with whom to share herself, but is not yet sure of those she is with. She is withholding herself from a full physical commitment until she is more secure in her surroundings.

The red shoes show that she is not yet at the end of her patience, but is a little more impatient at this time, requiring some indication of changes to come. The pointed toe shows that if others do not take up the reins, then she is prepared to do so for herself in the not too distant future.

The blue underwear indicates that emotional insecurities from her past make it difficult for her to trust others without proof that they mean what they say. It implies that she needs to be emotionally reassured of her physical direction before she can commit herself totally. On a more mundane level she is both able to and desires to be with other people, and is more prepared to venture out for a night on the town than stay at home and wash her hair.

She has emotional warmth to share with others, and needs them to recognise her for what she has to offer as a person rather than as an object of desire. She may be open to suggestions, but only those which offer her the emotional security that she still seeks whether she is already married or not.

If you were to meet her casually in the street and say hello she would respond in a pleasant manner but that is a far as it would go. This lady already has someone or something in mind, and if you don't fit the bill you would soon be told you have gone too far (red shoes). She is armed and ready to find an outlet for her emotional energy, but it has to be with that special person of her dreams, for anything less would sell her short. To others she would appear to be outwardly buoyant and happy, energetic and ready to respond and interact with others. Although this is so, there is a nagging doubt at the back of her mind that all is not yet what it should be in her life. To stabilise herself she is once again setting out to taste a degree of personal freedom in order that she may make that total link.

The subject's response to my interpretation
'I am in a funny mood. My boyfriend has asked me to move in and live with him, and while I feel that I do care for him, I am not sure that I want to commit myself to this sort of relationship. He can be very much his own man at times, and it's hard enough to get him away from his pals when we do go for a night out, and I don't want to become the woman stuck in the home. If I stay where I am I still have the freedom to go out as I please, which can make Paul more responsive to my needs, but I feel he may take me for granted if I move in with him.'

When asked if that was the only conflict she felt in her life at this time she replied.

'I want to get out more and see some of life before I settle down. We always seem to go to the same places and meet the same faces, and I would like to see a change in our social circle. Other than that, I am content to carry on working and enjoy my job as a hotel receptionist where I don't have the time to get bored, and enjoy working with the other people there. Though some of the customers are a pain, I always find something to smile at after. I just wish Paul would not try to rush me into something I might not be ready for.'

Comments
The subject was dressed in a manner which reflected how she felt about her circumstances at the time when she was coming to see a clairvoyant to help her make a decision she felt under pressure to make. The next day she may have worn a totally different combination of colours, but by then she may have changed her views about what she was about to do. The deeper meanings of the colours she wore did fit her circumstances at that time, though she infomed me that she is quite fond of

pink and white and wears it quite a lot. But perhaps the desire to find what she seeks is also a long-standing affair.

Case Two.

Subject Male
Age 43

Colours Worn

The subject was wearing a light brown suit with a pale yellow shirt and brown tie, his socks were black, as were his shoes, and he informed me that he wore no vest and dark red burgundy underpants. There was one large signet ring on the middle finger of the left hand and he did not wear a belt.

The Interpretation

The light brown suit shows that the subject outwardly needs to be recognised for his material achievements and steadfast reliability. His yellow shirt shows that he is both self-critical and critical of those around him, and needs a position of authority to feel emotionally secure.

The problem arises when we get to the black shoes and socks which neither fit into the colour scheme or the individual.

These indicate a secretive side to his future plans and physical direction, and would indicate that he is not all that he pretends to be. His burgundy underwear shows that he would like to be a lot more physically active than he is at this time, but more in a business manner than in the sexual sense (surrounded by brown).

The overall effect is that here we have a man who has had to force himself to take control of both his physical and emotional well-being. He is not totally happy with this, and desires some form of help or assistance, but cannot lose control or have others take the credit for what he feels he has achieved. He is seeking to build a material base from which he can expand into the emotional realms, but something is making him too logical in his application of his desires (yellow shirt). He believes in what he can hold in his hand, rather than on promises made, and would be better employed by someone else, though given a degree of trust and responsibility (black shoes and socks). He is seeking to build a stronger physical relationship with others, but has as yet not found an outlet for his sexuality as he feels that it is linked to what you have rather than what you are (burgundy underwear). He wants to be successful in what he applies himself to, and for others to recognise his success.

The Subject's Response

The subject told me that he bought the suit for a new job as office manager for a haulage firm some two years to reflect his recognition and responsibility at work. It was also the same suit he had worn for his divorce some 9 months previously when he said he was 'taken to the cleaners.' His feeling now of wanting to re-establish his material base stems from this. He also added that he had a new woman in his life, but that he was afraid to make any promises or project his relationship any further until he had consolidated his current desire to move away from the present job and area and begin life anew in the south of the country. (His hidden energy of the black shoes and socks — he has not told his current employers or his new friend or his intentions.) He does not yet feel that he wishes to remarry, and considers his present relationship to be mutual company (red underwear) though his own logic (yellow shirt) stops him from seeing what he really desires or allows him to give to others that part of himself which he really needs to express.

Comments

The subject in this case thought that all in his life was going well, but put too much emphasis on work rather than the home, which was the eventual cause of his broken marriage. Far from learning this lesson, he laid the blame for his material insecurity upon his ex-wife and set out bitterly on a path of material renewal. He is aware that this does not give him the emotional security he desires, but feels that from a firmer base he can attain what he seeks. Women in his life now are, in his own words, for mutual pleasure, which indicates his logical approach to relationships and his desire for a non-commital future. He is — if only he knew it — on the same self-destructive path that caused him his unhappiness in the past. He would be better off not trying to form new relationships, as he is at present unable to give a partner what they desire, only take what he needs when he needs it.

CONCLUSION

Colours can help us to understand how we each wish to be treated and will respond when shown a degree of understanding from those we associate with. The ball is now in your court. It's up to you how you pitch your colour vibration.

COLOURS IN TUNE

White is pure,
Red is quick,
Brown has wealth,
And black is slick.

Yellow puts thought,
Into Orange's ambition,
And with green you heal
All of blue's inhibitions.

Philosophise with purple
When you are alone,
But please keep some pink,
For a real happy home.

By Steven John

COLOURS IN LOVE AND ROMANCE

To test your reactions in romance and love simply select what you feel to be your favourite colour from the following list and read the relevant pages which will reflect your emotional mood at the time of the test.

A. White go to page 106
B. Red go to page 108
C. Pink go to page 109
D. Orange go to page 111
E. Yellow go to page 113
F. Green go to page 114
G. Blue go to page 116
H. Brown go to page 118
I. Purple go to page 119
J. Black go to page 120

This simple colour test can be used on a daily basis giving you an indication of your ability to interact with those that you have chosen to share your life with. The colour chosen reflects the stronger side of your emotional feelings at the time of selection and for that period of interaction. It should be used as a useful guide rather than a be-all-or-end-all as other colour vibrations around you effect the overall result.

White

If you selected white as your romantic colour then you have removed yourself from the wrongs or rights of your romantic situation. You are seeking the dreamed of situation, the perfect partner rather than the imperfect being most people are. You may be old fashioned in your views on romance and courtship as well as possessive of your chosen partner. You require to be admired and respected for what you are without taking the responsibility for what you are not. White is chaste and pure and will give of itself only to one at a time and then only when it has reassured itself that the taker's love is as pure or idealistic as its own.

Positive white in romance is as strict and stern with itself as it demands others be. Its moral ethics are usually at odds with the ever-changing society that it lives in but it is this opposition which brings an overall balance to the environment that we all must learn to cope with. White must lead rather than be led and it feels that it is responsible for the actions and morals of those with which it comes into contact. This can cause it to be picky about whom to associate with. White must learn to mix more with others rather than try to create singular relationships upon which all hopes are laid.

Outwardly clinical and cold to those that do not truly know them, whites are in fact the guardians of the morals of society and without their strong ethics, the world as we know it would crumble into the barbaric pagan past.

Negative white can become too dictatorial about the actions and morals of others, leading to a self imposed loneliness from which there is no escape as it constantly seeks the purity of mind which can never exist in the flesh.

Best Colours for Whites
White is not actually a colour but is in fact a carrier of all

other colours and has the ability to mix with all the other colours of the rainbow should it so desire. Only black has this same ability though on an opposite level. As black absorbs the colour shone into it, so white reflects the tone directed at it. White can reflect any colour vibration it desires. All it needs is the ambition or motivation to do so. If your partner chose white, you must learn to ask rather than demand and suggest rather than state. In so doing you will receive all that white has to offer.

Red

Red is a positive active vibration of a physical nature and if you selected this colour as an indicator of your romantic inclinations, then few will be able to keep pace with you or even desire to do so. Red is the colour of physical passion and not of true romance. Red's passion erupts like a volcano into love at first sight but can burn out into dull embers, realising that it was merely an infatuation that it has become bored with.

Positive red loves with every part of its being and with such intensity that others may find it to overpowering though it does tend to exist on a physical rather than emotional level. Red commits every part of itself and expects the same from associates.

Rash impulsive and adventurous are descriptions associated with the colour red, but so too is the ability to throw itself in at the deep end, committing totally both emotionally and physically. Red in romance craves excitement, variety and change, not necessarily in partnerships but definitely in surroundings and activities and it is only bordom that will cause a red romantic to look elsewhere for what he feels will stimulate him. Red is intensely passionate on the physical plane and will be open to most suggestions, with the motto "Don't knock it till you've tried it" resounding from its lips.

Red is an ardent lover who will go out of his or her way to please a chosen mate should the idea be appealing, but on the negative side reds can tend to be selfish, wanting to indulge only the things in which they find pleasure. Spontaneous as they are they also require a mate who can either keep pace with them or allow them a degree of personal freedom to experience the things which they feel the need to do. If your partner chose this colour to express his or her romantic inclinations, be warned they are possessive and require a total commitment and attention when you are in their company. They will be willing to co-operate with your ideas and suggestions but only if you respond with the same totality to theirs.

Best Colour Match for Red

Red is best suited to other reds which can match its energy and drive in romance or to black or white. Black is complimentary to red because it has the ability to absorb the energy which red is apt to project at given times, while white is able to reflect red's energy or soften it to the paler pink which is red's expression of true romantic energy. Other colours may appear to compliment red but the energy mix is neither as understanding nor as in tune with red's needs. Red should avoid blues and green but can mix with some browns.

Pink

Pink is, as far as we are concerned, the true colour of real romance combining within it the carrier spectrum and purity of the white vibration blended to the physical energy of red. It allows the rigid white energy to express itself through the physical action of red bringing together a balance of emotional and physical energy which has the ability to stand the test of time.

If you chose pink as an indicator of your romantic expression, then you are at heart a warm understanding individual capable of both giving and taking in romantic situations. You are a shoulder to cry on in your partner's time of need, but also capable of making them face up to self-pity and sorrow when you need to. You have the time, patience and loyalty to devote to your chosen mate in order that you may assist them through life's trials and as long as they recognise your unselfish efforts you will always be there in their time of need. As a pink romancer you do yourself require your partner to be open and demonstrative of their feelings towards you and will become offended if you feel that they withold either pleasure or pain from you, as yours is a partnership of caring and sharing, be it good or bad. Pink has a warm vibration that others seem to be drawn to in their hour of need and although it is capable of being ultra-supportive, this is only given when its trust and respect has been won. If your partner chose the colour pink you should think yourself lucky that you have found yourself an emotionally and physically supportive mate who will stand by you in your time of need and all they ask in return is that you notice what they do in support of you and show your appreciation and respect when the opportunity presents itself. Pink is the colour of true romance and you should make it a point to remember pink's anniversaries and special occasions as pink puts great store by these occasions. If you neglect or fail to show pink the love they show for you, it will be your own fault if you awake one morning and find that they have gone in search of what you failed to supply.

Pink's Best Colour Matches.
Pink has the ability to mix with all the colours of the spectrum and can give rather than take in emotional relationships. It does however excel with white and red in most circumstances, since it is originally a combination of the two. With yellow it becomes the colour of flesh and the logical expression of yellow never allows it full expression of its emotional feelings. It can help heal green and blue and teach brown to be more giving. It also has the ability to unlock the secret reserves of black.

Orange

Orange is not one of the better colours to choose when relating to your romantic capabilities. It combines the physical energy of red and the logical thought of yellow. Orange romantics need to sit down and plan their romantic times, and yet can never keep to their projected ambitions because they always have to react to circumstances or events. The desire to control their romantic direction fails to take into account the reaction of the colour vibration that they have chosen to mix with. This always means that their plans were useless and they then have to live on their nervous energy which can lead to insecurity and self-destruction. Orange is a seeker of pleasure and assumes that which it finds pleasurable will also be pleasurable for its chosen mate. This, however, is not usually the case and most orange romantics will go through some form of trouble or strife before they find the stability and security that they really seek. Orange romantics can become overly possessive and assertive in their relationships, but it is this desire to control their romantic circumstances and avoid conflict which can lead them upon the very path they try so hard to avoid. Orange romantics can go between moments of great joy, elation and happiness to the extremes of self-pity, sorrow and depression and can find the balance between the two only through experience.

Negative orange can be self-destructive to extremes, feeling that others should share their feelings of sorrow and unhappiness. They are liable to try to drag others to their own level when feeling sorry for themselves. Their saviour is that they have the ability to pick themselves up very quickly after knocks, and although quick-tempered, they are just as quick to forgive and forget after the event. Orange romantics tend to look for stronger partners, never quite realising why they do so. It is in fact an inner desire for someone else to take the strain of controlling them as they sometimes doubt their own ability to control themselves.

They do in fact not need either a dominant nor submissive partner, more likely one who can move with them between the two levels upon which they function.

Best Matches for Orange

Orange is best understood by another orange, both reds and yellows have common vibrations being the creators of orange but we feel they would tend to bring out the extremes of moods be they good or bad that orange types can experience. Black is a good colour for orange being able to absorb its energies while white though able to dilute the energy is not really compatible with it. Blue may understand it but green will always be unsettled by it. Brown can enhance orange giving it direction and purpose. Purple is out of tune.

Yellow is the bright gay colour of communications and the thought process. If you chose yellow as an indicator of your romantic vibrations then you are indicating your desire or preference to outdoor activities and or intellectually stimulating partnerships. We state outdoor but not in the sense of great physical activity more in the inquisitive desire to explore the unknown. Orange romantics may like to travel and experience the world before they settle down and of all the colour vibrations this is the one most likely to marry away from home or to someone foreign to their culture. In the romantic situation you can have no secrets from a yellow type though they tend to be more mentally stimulated then physically you can be sure that they excel at whatever they put their minds to.

Yellow romantics tend to formulate plans and work towards a goal, their courtships can be long before an eventual bonding but they are rarely boring. Yellow romantics tend to talk you into the situation that they desire to see you in and it is usually long past the finishing post before you realise that you were ever in a race. Yellow needs to keep some form of control over its emotions and you may never see the real person within this type unless you take the time and patience to seek what they have to offer.

Yellow romantics are at their best when in the public eye as they have an ardent desire to show off to the rest of society what they feel they have achieved be it on a romance of business level. Many yellow romantics marry through travel or work and if the two can be combined then so much the better. Negative yellow can be very dictorial about its affections and just like the sun which rises above us bringing light and life yellow romantics need the praise for any favours it condescends to grant you. Yellow can be the bringer of life to a desert oasis or the scorched sand which surrounds it and it is this complete opposite of types that we can encounter with this vibration, either the giver or the taker.

Best Matches for Yellow

Red and orange can complement yellow but tend to bring out one extreme or the other in the vibration while white is a bad mix creating a logical machine. Pink is capable of mixing with all colours but is not at its best with yellow while green simply loves to expand under yellows direction. Blue is a vibration which yellow seeks to understand and the two can make a good match but brown is one of its better complimentary vibrations creating growth and stability in a partnership.

Purple and yellow is either very good or very bad as each relate to thought processes but on material and spiritual levels which often fail to mix well. Black can absorb all that yellow throws at it but never seems to respond in the way in which yellow feels adequate.

Best matches for yellow are green and brown.

Green

Green is the colour of material healing and natural expansion and if you selected green as your colour of romantic inclinations then you are seeking a partnership of physical and mental balance with neither either controlling or failing in its equality. Green is a neutral colour encomposing both the warm intellect of green and the cold colour and emotional intensity of blue. The adage blue and green should not be seen is in our

opinion incorrect as the two colour vibrations complement each other being the physical and mental healing
vibrations. When you chose green as a colour of romance you were expressing your desire to leave the
field of romantic combat and settle down to a normal
passive and content relationship. Most people who
select this colour may have been divorced or experienced some form of emotional or romantic trauma in
their past which they have faced up to and are trying to
put behind them in order that they may start life anew.
Green is a rich colour of growth and expansion and
romantic greens wish to spread their wings and experience the joys which they feel that they have deprived
themselves of in the past.

Romantic greens have a sympathetic ear for their
partners feeling that they have experienced whatever it
is that their chosen soul mate is going through and try
to lighten their mates load with their past experiences.

Greens neutrally allows them to be privaled with the
inner thoughts of their mates as they seem to bring out
that trust in those that surround them. Negative green
on the other hand is still going through that period of
self healing and can be an emotional liability to their
partners constantly requiring the reassurance that positive green is able to give so easily. If your partner chose
this vibrational colour then you have a life time loyal
partner who if given trust and reassurance that you will
make it in the end will stick by you through thick and
thin. Green romance vibrations have the ability to forgive and forget an injustice but never take them for
granted as you can push them only so hard then they
will cut of your stability in search of one who appreci-
ates their efforts.

Best Matches for Green

Despite the adage "Blue and green should not be seen", it is our opinion that these two colours complement each other perfectly. Yellow is a part of green and has some compatibility, though not as much. Red annoys green with its constant demands for change, while pink is able to respond to green's desires. Green grows out of brown in the long term, while purple has too high a spiritual vibration for green to understand. White dilutes green away from its true direction but is not an overly bad match. Green should, however, avoid all shades of orange.

Blue

Blue is the colour of emotional intensity as a romantic indicator and those who selected this colour require a relationship that has lots of emotional reassurance, otherwise you will seek it elsewhere should you ever gain the confidence. Of all the colour vibrations, blue is one prefers to stay at home and create its own pleasure. Blues are imaginative, though insecure, lovers, requiring responsive and emotionally demonstrative partners who constantly cuddle, fondle and reassure them. Positive blue is extremely loyal and will never forgive those who misuse or abuse the trust they put into their partnerships. Negative blue is never quite sure it has found its imaginary perfect partner and never truly stops looking for him or her or testing the one it has for loyalty. Romantic blues can enjoy a night in with someone they love just as much as a night out for they believe the person they are with is more important than where they are. They are very intense people which many other colour vibrations find hard to respond to with equal power. A blue is a very imaginative individual and whereas that can be very creative in some circumstances, it can, in its negative context, be very destructive, as their fear-imaginary or otherwise of what may happen can stop them from enjoying what they actually have.

Romantic blue has the ability to give when need be and for great periods of time under adverse conditions, as long as it is sure the taker is worthy of what it has to offer and eventually rewards it for its efforts. Negative romantic blue is emotionally selfish in the sense that it desires constant attention and the reassurance that it has made the correct romantic choice. This inhibits it from ever really achieving what it set out to build. Most romantic blues tend to be great mothers and fathers, desiring to give to their children all the things which they feel that they lacked in their childhood, be they physical gifts or emotional security. Romantic blue can be very insecure and irrational at times, and requires a developed understanding from its chosen mate. Once this is achieved, however, you have the foundations for a life-long partnership through thick and thin.

Best Matches for Blue

Best match for blue is green. Red can be good as long as he doesn't push too hard, and purple is compatible with most blues because of a spiritual ability to understand each other. Black is capable of absorbing blue's periods of self-pity but white should be avoided as it leaves a feeling of emptiness. Orange takes from blue and is not a good match, but brown can give blue the emotional base to build upon.

Those of you who chose brown as an indicator of your romantic abilities can appear aloof and detached from such mundane things as romance, or so others think. The brown soil in Nature may look bare and barren, yet waits only for the right conditions before it bursts into colours and vibrations once the setting is correct. So it is with romantic browns who tend to require a degree of financial security before they feel they can totally let themselves be drawn into the emotional whirlpool of romance. Many romantic browns are self-assured as it is the colour vibration which learns best from other peoples mistakes rather than its own and tends to be set only on certainties rather than black high odds outsiders. Romantic browns have a depth of wealth and pleasure to offer their chosen partner should they ever find the equal they seek. However, they tend to go for those of their own type, preferring a quieter path until they get a little older. Then, they try to attain all they feel they missed in the past when they feel the time was not right. Romantic browns on the negative side can be workaholics, always trying to achieve financial stability and success and yet never content with what they have achieved. They feel they should accomplish just one more deal before they settle down, which could mean they miss the boat.

Romantic browns need to learn that too much work makes for a dull lover. They may intend to build dream homes and lives, but may never actually get around to it because they are so wrapped up in their work. Browns can be a very generous and caring spouses and if they ever find what they truly seek, then there is nothing they would not endevour to give those they love. Romantic brown really comes into its own in its mid 30's when it has usually built its material base and is able to concentrate its great energies into its romantic life. Romantic browns tend to be mentally a little more mature than their contemporaries, and yet, emotionally, they may still be children at heart. It is the childhood dreams that romantic brown works so hard to fulfill.

Best Matches for Brown
Brown can get on with the logical yellow vibration as both have ambitions and a similar thought processes. Red tends to harden brown but can make it a little bit more able to commit itself in situations that it would normally avoid. Black will take all brown has to offer, be it good or bad, but white wants more attention than it thinks brown types give. Green grows out of brown in the long term, yet always returns for advice, so this combination is better for friends rather than lovers. Orange can be good or bad and blue is average.

Purple

Purple as a romantic colour vibration is really out of tune with the society in which most of us live. It is the colour vibration of the philosopher and the higher mind, as well as royalty and the religious sects. Its vibration is better directed through the ability to love a good book, or good or humanitarian concepts, rather than through the baser physical plane. If you selected purple as an indicator of your romantic inclination then you are more likely to enjoy a solitude rather than the company of others. Positive purple is chaste, pure, spiritual and caring and would be more likely to occur in religious sects, such the Mormons than in the average man. Negative purple, however, uses the baser red energy from within itself to satisfy its feeling of self-pleasure, self-gratification and lust, for which there is no end or beginning. It feels that it is correct and right in its actions, as others have learned by the pleasure of its company, can be intolerable but even to the point of being depressive. Romantic purple if expressed on this plan, would be a do-gooder always sacrificing its own desires for the desires of those around them. It is not, we feel, a suitable colour vibration upon which to build a physical relationship.

If you chose this colour, you may be better off away from the responsibilities of relationships with other individuals, and wed instead to the church or relief agency on the positive side, or to yourself on the negative side. Romantic purple is a colour vibration that has not yet been born in the world we know and live in and is perhaps best left for future generations to unravel and explain, if they can.

Best Matches for Purple

Red and blue combine to make purple, so if this vibration is chosen then these are at least composites of it. Black has many hidden sides to it and could be compatible. White has the ability to water down its higher ideal, but it is our opinion if you chose this colour you are discontented with your romantic situation and are trying to find a new direction for either projecting or hiding your romantic feelings.

Black

Black carries the secretive side of romance. Like a sponge, it absorbs it environment and becomes what is necessary for its own survival. Black as a romantic indicator can mean that the chooser has something to hide from their partner, that they may lack a degree of security and stability or simply that they like to tease you into seeing for yourself what is there.

Romantic black has a desire to experience all that the world has to offer and yet needs to be led where it treads by others. Do not be fooled by romantic black's attitudes, for he can be as pleasant as a summer's morning or as bleak as a winter's gale. Romantic black is seeking the answer to his own questions and desires, but needs to experience them through others to test their validity, as he is never quite able to trust his own opinion.

The black night hides a mass of uncertainties, noises and riches and whoever ventures into the unknown will find either adventure and wealth or a precipice from which he may fall. Romantic black is seeking himself and although capable of interacting with others, he will give only what he has received, no more and sometimes even less. Romantic black is on a quest of self-discovery and it is not until he has found himself that he can learn to share it with others. Black may be considered by some a sexual colour, but sex in itself is superficial and only a part of a relationship, not its be-all-and-end-all. We associate black with sexuality because, as a species, we tend to make secret and inhibited an act which is Nature's gift of the dusk. To share sexuality totally and freely with a loved one is the only salvation from an incomplete life which many black romantics live. Romantic black likes to see itself as the hunted, and only from this point of view can it feel itself accepted for what it really is, rather than for what others want it to be.

Best Matches for Black

Black is a carrier of all colours and is capable of interacting with them all on one level or another. However, the warm colours such as pink, yellow and red would give black more of the excitement that it always seems to be seeking. Blue and green can help to heal black's inner hurts and regenerate it, but brown is not a good match other than in a business partnership type of romance. White turns black into grey, which makes it commit itself too soon, though purple could help black to understand why it is as it is.

The Colour Test Author's Note

The colour vibrations listed in reference to your romantic inclinations should be referred to only as guide to your inner thoughts, desires and ambitions, the obstacles you may encounter and the abilities you may possess. It is however only one of the colour vibrations which effects your overall existence, and should be treated, as was intended, as an indicator, not as a firm rule.

INDEX

If this book was helpful, there are others by the same author which you should know about . . .

I'VE GOT YOUR LUCKY NUMBER
Understand its vibration and impact on both your personality and relationships.

Numbers do have a part to play in character analysis. Whether you are using astrology, palmistry or tarot cards to discover your inner-most secrets – they are all based on numerology.

With the help of this book, it is easy to calculate your own personal birth number (or those of your family) and to learn much from the analysis/interpretation which the author provides for you.

Steven Culbert has widely researched birth numbers and he sets out in this book to familiarise the reader with the principles of the ancient art of numerology, more fancifully known as metaphysical mathematics.

ISBN 0-572-01398-1   £2.99 net

THE RIGHT NAME FOR BABY
Reinforce the personal vibrations for a more positive future.

In metaphysical mathematics we learn that our birth number produces vibrations which are with us for life. Now you can complement these vibrations; reinforce them; protect them.

If you are about to select 2 or 3 names for your baby, doesn't it make sense to make a decision that will enhance the future? Of course it does.

Here are the vibrations of hundreds of names from which you may choose. Or, alternatively, the principles and workings with which to test the name you *think* you would like to use.

ISBN 0-572-01430-9   £3.50 net

**Available from your local bookseller or newsagent.
In case of difficulty contact:
W. FOULSHAM & CO. LTD.,
Yeovil Road, Slough, SL1 4JH, England.**